The Miracle of Mark

A TOWER
BOOK

The Miracle of Mark

A Study in the Gospel

ROY A. HARRISVILLE

AUGSBURG PUBLISHING HOUSE
MINNEAPOLIS, MINNESOTA

THE MIRACLE OF MARK

Library of Congress Catalog Card No. 67-11725

Manufactured in the United States of America

Foreword

A tower has both height and strength. Grounded in a firm foundation, it provides the opportunity for a full-range perspective and soaring vision. It was in a tower that Luther had the shattering experience of grace which began the Reformation with its insights into the Gospel of God and new freedoms for man.

Volumes in the Tower Book series aspire to this image. They seek to serve the curious and reflective Christian by examining the varied themes of God and man in clear, concise, and interesting (perhaps even sparkling) ways. Committed to the biblical faith, the various authors explore great ideas, reflect on the application of the faith to daily life, transmit the wisdom of inspiring thinkers in the past, suggest new strategy for the church in the world, and open up the Scriptures as honestly and competently as they can.

Each author is different and writes from his own "tower" and in his own style. You, the reader, read against the background of your own experience, of course.

Being a Christian in the modern age is an exciting enterprise. It requires both diligence and knowledge. For this task, we all need the help and counsel of others.

Take and read.

And joy to you!

Kent S. Knutson
Editor, Tower Books

Preface

This little book has no specific destination, no particular reader in mind. It is a non-technical piece written for whoever will read it. If by chance some student of theology should light upon it, let me acknowledge indebtedness to two contemporary scholars who furnished me the stimulus to treat the subject as I did: first, to Rudolf Bultmann of Marburg for his suggestion that Mark's Gospel is a combination of Hellenistic preaching with the tradition of the story of Jesus; second, to Willi Marxsen of Münster whose volume *Der Evangelist Markus* is one of the first in our time to concentrate all its attention upon the theology of Mark.

In our generation, the Gospel of Mark is undergoing new evaluation at the hands of many a biblical scholar. For example, the intimate connection once seen between Mark and Paul is being challenged, partly because that connection was essential to a school of thought which emerged in the 19th, was dominant at the beginning of the 20th century, and whose method is presently being subjected to intense criticism. In one sense, Mark's Gospel has become a kind of "Pork Chop Hill" over which opposing systems and methods of interpretation join battle, suffer defeat, and regroup to do battle again. Each system, each method, struggles to fix its flag on its soil. It will be clear to the practiced eye that my discussion reflects allegiance to a view which tends to emphasize the proclamatory character of the New Testament. And yet, if my assent to the evaluation of our "preacher" as weaving together the Hellenistic preaching about Christ and the historical tradition of Jesus is correct, Mark himself may show us all the way toward preserving what is most valuable in the opposing methods of New Testament interpretation and at the same time introduce a new era of biblical study. One thing, at least, is certain: In any future examination of the New Testament, the individuality and creativity of its authors must receive larger place than is customarily given them, and to that extent the argument of this little book may retain some validity.

If this piece encourages a new reading of the Gospel and a new comprehension of its place within the New Testament canon, some of the anxiety over having once more merely scratched the surface will have been lifted.

Roy A. Harrisville

Contents

1.

Giving the Preacher His Due

The Marcan Priority

Long ago the world of scholars gave to Mark a priority in the history of Christian literature. But it still remains the least read and least used Gospel in the church. A quick glance at the pastor's list of preaching texts assigned him for Sundays in the year will indicate the lack of appreciation from which Mark has suffered since the time of Saint Augustine in the 5th century. The reason for this disuse is clear—it was once assumed that the Gospels were composed in the order in which they appear in our New Testament, and that Mark therefore was merely a poor man's version of Matthew. But it is one of the surest results of the historical study of the Gospels that Mark was written first and that it set the pattern for other Gospels, whether in or outside the New Testament. If you were to place Matthew, Mark, and Luke side by side, verse by verse, you would quickly appreciate the similarity of their contents. And perhaps you would see, as did the pioneers of our modern view of the relationship between the first three Gospels, that it is indeed the Gospel of Mark which provides the other two with their "backbone."

Popular Opinion

Agreed, then, that of our first three Gospels Mark deserves the priority in time, how ought we to value it? For one thing, it is shorter than Matthew and Luke. It contains no narrative of Jesus' birth; it lacks Matthew's Sermon on the Mount, and those grand parables of the lost sheep, coin, and prodigal son in Luke 15 are absent from it. The only detailed narrative in Mark is the Passion story. The rest gives the impression of being a cluster of isolated pieces, strung together with such picayune devices as "and," "as," "again," "when," "in those days," and what-not. If Mark's outline provides the Gospels of Matthew and Luke with their "backbone," that backbone gives more the appearance of a series of slipped discs than of a real spine. Indeed, since 1919 a goodly number of scholars have viewed Mark more as a newspaper makeup man than as a genuine, died-in-the-wool evangelist with any kind of point of view. Matthew has real structure, at least the kind of structure we expect from a proper book—it is divided into five almost equal parts with an introduction and a conclusion. Luke and Acts as well enjoy a carefully planned sequence—the "time of Jesus" and the "time of the church" form its two distinct parts. But what sense is to be made of Mark which paints one rapid picture after another and then suddenly comes to an end with the telling of the women's fright at hearing the angel of the resurrection? (The rest of the final chapter is a later addition as the RSV indicates.) It may be because of this sudden screeching to a halt that Mark has since ancient times been called Colybodactylus—"stubby-fingered."

On the other hand, there is little doubt that in the final analysis our evaluation of Mark rests upon prejudice. Because of their continual use in preaching and

Bible study, Matthew and Luke have become second-nature to us. In the use of the Bible, as with all other things, that which is known is usually to be preferred. Other books which have an intrinsic value far beyond what is known are neglected. Christmas would not be Christmas, Epiphany would not be Epiphany without the second chapters of Luke and of Matthew. But if during Passion Week the Christian community had been exposed for a century or two to Mark, especially chapters 14 and 15, Bach would no doubt have composed a St. Mark rather than a St. Matthew Passion and the comparable chapters in Matthew and Luke would have fallen into disuse and hence into disfavor. There is, of course, one Christian festival with which the reading of Mark is associated—Ascension Day, celebrated only by the strictest within the liturgical communions of Christendom!

Mark: A Sermon

Our original question had to do with putting a proper value upon Mark, however highly we may regard the other Gospels. Whether or not a priority of quality should be added to the priority in time given this "first" Gospel can only be decided by the reader when the last period has been put. To prod him to such a decision is the purpose of this little book.

The first fact to face is that Mark is not a biography. This does not mean there are no biographical details in the Gospel. At best, however, they are minimal. The description of the hero, glimpses into his inner life, his moods and attitudes, which we expect from a modern biography, are all but totally absent from Mark. The author's purpose is not to write the story of Jesus *a la* Fulton Oursler or movie-producer George Stevens.

Nor is the Gospel a history in any modern sense of that term. Again, this does not mean that Mark is not interested in recording historical fact. If we allow the Gospel writer an integrity equal to what we accord any serious writer, it is reasonable to assume that he views much of what he writes as true to life. Yet, his penchant for lumping together various kinds of narrative and speech material—Jesus' disputes with the ecclesiastical authorities, for example, or the parables—indicates that his purpose is not, as in Luke's case, to narrate the events surrounding the life and career of Jesus in any chronological fashion. His method may be compared to that of Matthew for whom a scheme or peculiar point of view dominates the arrangement of his Gospel.

The best way by which to describe the Gospel of Mark is to call it a *sermon*, the kind of sermon which audiences in the first century of our era customarily heard from Christian evangelists and orators. According to one old father of the church, Papias of Hierapolis (A.D. 150), Mark's Gospel is a translation and transcription of the sermons of Peter by John Mark, early companion of Paul and Silas (cf. Acts 12:12, 25). Though Papias' statement comes to us only second-hand, via the historian Eusebius, and is capable of a thousand and one interpretations, it at least indicates that the Gospel's sermonic character was recognized from earliest times. Actually, the word "Gospel" or "Evangel," perhaps first appropriated by the Apostle Paul from Roman emperor worship (according to which any event connected with the life of the Caesar or a decree from Caesar was regarded as "gospel," as "good news"), denotes first of all a proclamation or sermon, and only secondarily a writing. Mark, thus, is a sermon, congealed in writing, an appeal to the hearer-reader to surrender himself in trust and obedience to the Figure who strides through his pages like a Colossus.

Back and Forth in the Gospel

Now a sermon must have structure, a scheme giving to it unity and coherence, something into which the hearer may sink his teeth and hence remember. And despite the tendency among many of its readers to see in the Gospel nothing but a potpourri of disconnected scenes arranged willy-nilly, the book does have such a scheme and thus such a unity.

Among others, the *death-motif* gives unity to the Gospel. When we read backward from the crucifixion narrative in chapters 14 and 15 (incidentally, the only chapters in the Gospel in which meticulous attention is given to detail) to the opening chapters of the Gospel, it is clear that the death of Jesus forms a constant, unbroken refrain. Chapter 13, the so-called "Little Apocalypse," with its dramatic picture of the final summing up on earth and in heaven, describes the persecution awaiting Christ's faithful during the interim in precisely those terms in which his own trial and execution are described—they will be "brought to trial and delivered up." In chapter 12, the death-theme appears not only in the parable of the vineyard in which the tenants beat the owner's servants and kill his son, but in the attempt of Jesus' enemies to arrest him "for they perceived that he had told the parable against them," as well as to "entrap him in his talk" (v. 12; cf. vv. 13 ff.). In chapter 11, the highest ecclesiastical authorities seek a way to destroy him. Chapter 10 marks the third of Jesus' "Passion predictions" (a chapter in which Jesus speaks ominously of his coming "baptism," vv. 38-39); Mark 9 contains the second and chapter 8 the first. In chapter 8 Jesus also describes discipleship in terms of "taking up" one's "cross" and following him, v. 34.

The death-motif is less evident in chapter 7, though it throws its shadow in the opening lines alluding to the "spies" from Jerusalem. The death of the Baptist in chapter 6 is a grim omen of what is to follow, and is consequently one of the most detailed narratives in the Gospel (cf. 6:17 ff). Chapter 5, with its references to tombs, drowning, sickness, and death (the daughter of Jairus), is almost totally devoted to the death-theme. The parable of the sower in chapter 4 treats of rejection and unbelief—"other seed fell among thorns and the thorns grew up and choked it, and it yielded no grain"—even on the part of his own company (cf. vv. 13, 38 ff.). The name of Judas "who betrayed him" first appears in chapter 3 (v. 19); in this chapter are also described the plots of the Pharisees and Herodians against Jesus (v. 6; cf. v. 2). The bridegroom parable in chapter 2 speaks of a time of fasting when the bridegroom is removed from his friends (v. 20), and in chapter 1 the destinies of Jesus and the Baptist are linked, first by Mark's peculiar choice of terms to describe the activity of John, terms normally reserved for a description of Jesus' career, and also by the word used to tell of John's arrest, the very same used of Pilate's crucifixion of Jesus in chapter 15 (cf. v. 15).

Beginning with the tempest of chapters 14 and 15 and reading backward, it is easy to see that though the storm may be only a ripple in the pond in chapter 1, the signals are there, the clouds have begun to gather. Like an overture in which all themes are sounded in the opening bars and wait only for their inevitable climax, Mark's Gospel at the outset strikes the death-note, quietly, ever so indistinctly, but with each succeeding chapter adds a bit of volume until all the fury of hell breaks loose in that agonizing cry: "My God, my God, why hast thou forsaken me?"

But this death-motif is more than a constant refrain first softly struck, then ending in a thundering crescendo. We already noted the influence of the account of Jesus' Passion upon the description of the Baptist's career and fate in chapter 1. Beyond this, the account of the death of Jesus can be shown to have influenced the shape as well as the content of other parts of the Gospel. For example, let us look for a moment at the sequence in the "Passion predictions" of chapters 8, 9, and 10—"must suffer . . . be rejected . . . be killed, and after three days rise again" (8:31); "will be delivered into the hands of men, and they will kill him; and when he is killed, after three days he will rise" (9:31); "the son of man will be delivered to the chief priests and the scribes, and they will condemn him to death, and deliver him to the Gentiles; and they will mock him, and spit upon him, and scourge him, and kill him; and after three days he will rise" (10:33-34).

Some raise the suspicion that Mark has read back into Jesus' prophecies the later account of his trial and death. They state that the predictions correspond so completely in language, style, and sequence to the actual events—cf. the prediction of chapter 10 with its references to such minute details as the Gentiles' (Romans') mocking, spitting, and scourging—that they have more the appearance of "prophecies after the event" than of real predictions.

Jesus' utterances concerning the future in chapter 13 have such striking parallels in the Passion story that we cannot avoid concluding that much of the so-called apocalyptic material is actually intended by Mark to have its echo, if not its fulfillment, in the Good Friday scene. In chapter 13 the word "to deliver up" is used three times of the community (vv. 9, 11, and 12) and in chapter 14 seven times of Jesus' betrayal (vv. 10, 11, 18, 21, 41, 42, and 44); in chapter 13 Jesus says of the coming of the Son of man that no one knows the "hour" (v. 32) and in chapter 14 he prays that the "hour" might pass from him (v. 35); in chapters 13 and 14 the night is divided into the four Roman watches (13:35; 14:17, 30, 72; cf. also 15:1), for Mark an unusual attention to time. Darkness is foretold in chapter 13:24 and darkness covers the earth in 15:33. The destruction of the temple is predicted in 13:2 and in 15 the temple veil is rent from top to bottom (v. 38). In chapters 13, 14, and 15 the admonition to "watch" is most frequent. (13:34, 35, 37; 14:34, 37, 38; cf. also the admonitions to "take heed" in 13:5, 9, 23, 33). Finally, the chapter and verse divisions in the ancient lectionaries or "altar books" give every reason to believe that the early church read chapter 13 as the introduction to the Passion history.

We are not about to deny that Jesus divined his ultimate fate or that he predicted the future. We merely point out that the Passion narrative is so central for Mark that its language, style, and arrangement have materially influenced the rest of his Gospel—further evidence for the unity and coherence of his "sermon." From this point of view, the Gospel of Mark is indeed, as one 19th century author put it, a Passion story "with a rather lengthy introduction."

But there is also a *forward movement* in Mark's Gospel, however loosely connected the scenes. Though, as noted above, that close attention to detail which marks modern story-writing appears only in the Passion narrative, there are places in the Gospel in which the author is at pains to preserve a narrative sequence. For example, Mark takes care to note that the ministry of Jesus does not coincide with that of the Baptist but follows hard after it—"Now after John was arrested, Jesus came into Galilee, preaching the Gospel of God" (1:14). Much more important, however, is the fact that Peter's confession at Caesarea Philippi ("You are the Christ," 8:29) forms a kind of watershed, dividing Jesus' ministry into two rather distinct phases. In the first seven chapters of the Gospel, Jesus carries on his activity in more or less hidden fashion—the demons are not allowed to acknowledge him publicly (1:25, 34; 3:12); the healed leper is enjoined to silence (1:44); Jesus speaks to the crowds in parables, explaining them only to his disciples (4:11-12, 33-34); he "strictly charges" the audience at the raising of Jairus' daughter "that no one should know this" (5:43); he travels incognito in Tyre and Sidon (7:24); the healing of the deaf-mute is to be kept a secret (7:36). Now this injunction to silence is not always obeyed.[1] The man possessed in chapter 5 proclaims "how much Jesus had done for him" (5:20). Five thousand are witness to his bounty at the feeding (6:44). He is unable to remain hidden in Tyre and Sidon (7:25, 36). And following Peter's confession, Jesus on occasion repeats his command to silence (8:30; 9:9) and travels incognito (9:30). But the events following Caesarea Philippi are for the most part public and justify our viewing Peter's confession as the "hinge" of the Gospel, separating a period of more or less secret activity from a later public ministry, climaxing in the events of Good Friday and Easter.

The influence of the Passion story upon the remainder of the book and the movement toward Caesarea Philippi and events beyond it give to Mark's Gospel its distinctive "backward-forward" character, a trait the reader must recognize in order to grasp the uniqueness of the Gospel's structure.

Warp and Woof

Now a sermon obviously has not only shape but also substance. What kind of flesh does Mark give to his skeleton? What "ax" does he "grind"? For centuries, Christians have been concerned to describe the points of view of the various Gospel writers. One of the earliest descriptions is that of Irenaeus. Taking as his text Revelation 4:7, and arguing that four Gospels and only four were intended from the beginning of time, the second-century church father writes:

> For the cherubim have four faces, and their faces are images of the activity of the Son of God. For the first living creature, it says, was like a lion, signifying his active and princely and royal character; the second was like an ox, showing his sacrificial and priestly order; the third had the face of a man, indicating very clearly his coming in human guise; and the fourth was like a flying eagle, making plain the giving of the Spirit who broods over the Church.[2]

Thus, for Irenaeus, John wrote of the Word become man, Luke emphasized Jesus' priestly role, Matthew dealt with him as man, and Mark accented the importance of prophecy. There are few cathedrals of Europe which do not contain a stained-glass window in which these four figures of the lion, ox, man, and eagle are not set to denote the four evangelists. Since Irenaeus, the attempts at such description have been legion.

Naturally, this volume will attempt to add to the thousands already current still one more description of the content of Mark. But rather than merely giving my opinion, supporting it by way of a few examples, and in grasshopper fashion proceeding to some kind of verse-by-verse, chapter-by-chapter interpretation of the text of Mark, I shall confine myself throughout to persuading the reader to my description of Mark's point of view by applying that description to the Gospel as a whole. Then, after the reader has gone the entire route with me, he may judge for himself whether or not the description and its application have any force.

The thesis of this study is first of all that the Gospel of Mark is a "sermon" which has as its main theme the *kind*[3] of material we find in Paul's "hymn" in Philippians:

> Have this mind among yourselves, which you have in Christ Jesus, who, though he was in the form of God, did not count equality with God a thing to be grasped, but emptied himself, taking the form of a servant, being born in the likeness of men. And being found in human form he humbled himself and became obedient unto death, even death on a cross. Therefore God has highly exalted him and bestowed on him the name which is above every name, that at the name of Jesus every knee should bow, in heaven and on earth and under the earth, and every tongue confess that Jesus Christ is Lord, to the glory of God the Father (Phil. 2:5-10).

That is, part of Mark's theme is the *type*[3] of affirmation which Christians converted by Paul or of Paul's frame of mind would hear or compose.

Such "hymns" as Philippians 2:5-10 are first of all "Hellenistic," that is, they originate outside Palestine among Greek-speaking peoples, and have a certain similarity to the statements which the devotees of heathen religions made about their gods. This is natural, since Christians in Greece, for example, could hardly afford to manufacture an entirely new religious vocabulary if they expected to speak intelligibly to their pagan contemporaries! In all such hymns and confessions the themes of descent-humiliation and ascent-exaltation are to the fore. Philippians 2:5-10, however, is by no means the only "Hellenistic" gospel incorporated in the writings of Paul. In the Letter to the Romans the same themes occur: "descended from David according to the flesh . . . designated Son of God in power according to the Spirit of holiness by his resurrection from the dead" (1:3-4; cf. 6:3 f. and 10:9). They appear in the 15th chapter of 1 Corinthians, perhaps the earliest Hellenistic gospel of all—"Christ died . . . was buried . . . was raised on the third day . . . appeared to Cephas . . . to the twelve . . . ." (15:3-5)—as well as in the apostles' sermons recorded in Acts (cf. 2:22-24; 3:13-15; 10:37-41; 13:26-31). But because of its all-inclusiveness, the "Christ-hymn" of Philippians 2 (a "hymn" Paul did not compose but found already in use among Greek Christians and appropriated for his own purpose) provides the best example of a "Hellenistic" gospel. One possible exception is that other great hymn to the Christ in Colossians 1:15-20, which, however, does not contain the ascent-exaltation theme.

If such material as we encounter in the "Christ-hymn" of Philippians forms the "warp," the tradition of the sayings and doings of Jesus forms the "woof" of Mark's Gospel. By virtue of its embracing the Palestinian tradition about Jesus, Mark's Gospel takes on a graphic character in contrast to the purely formal and conceptual nature of the "gospel" in Hellenistic circles. Mark undoubtedly found this Palestinian material in scattered form, or at best in small "blocks" of related sayings or incidents. He does not, however, leave his material in this form, but arranges it by subject matter. For example, the majority of Jesus' verbal battles with his enemies are noted in 2:1—3:6; the parable materials are limited principally to chapter 4, the apocalyptic material to chapter 13, etc. Mark thus connects the two strands of primitive Christian tradition—the Hellenistic and the Palestinian. Indeed, Mark's "sermon" is so unmistakably tinctured by a Semitic coloring that some have insisted that the Gospel is largely a translation of Palestinian, Aramaic (Jesus' mother tongue) originals. There is no doubt that in some sense Mark's Gospel is based upon Aramaic sources, whether oral or written. But the net result of his work—the weaving together of the Hellenistic and the Palestinian strands—is altogether due to the originality of our preacher. It is this fusion of the two traditions which helps to make the Gospel of Mark a "gospel," a proclamation.

2.

The Sermon

Colossus

He was in the form of God (Phil. 2:6a).

Keeping in mind that Mark's concern was not for chronological sequence,[1] we proceed now to a topical examination of his Gospel in light of the thesis proposed. Turning to the first strophe or line of the Christ-hymn, it is first of all clear that Mark's favorite designation for Jesus is "Son of God." The title appears in the superscription-summary of chapter 1: "The beginning of the gospel of Jesus Christ, the Son of God." The voice at his baptism announces, "Thou art my beloved Son" (1:11), and at his transfiguration declares, "This is my beloved Son" (9:7). The unclean spirits fall down before him and cry, "I know who you are, the Holy One of God" (1:24); "You are the Son of God" (3:11), or "Son of the Most High God" (5:7).[2]

At his trial Jesus is asked, "Are you the Christ, the Son of the Blessed?" and answers, "I am" (14:62), and at his crucifixion the centurion announces, "Truly this man was a son of God!" (15:39), a cry which complements the confession of Peter in 8:29. But perhaps even with Mark that title "Son of God" does not carry the pay-load we usually assign to it in the Nicene Creed—"Very God of Very God, Begotten, not made, Being of one substance with the Father; By whom all things were made." Some assert that for Mark the title "Son of God" is the normal equivalent of "Messiah," a term which carried no intimations of deity. Others suggest that for our preacher Jesus was the "adopted" Son of God, i.e. that he "became" the Son of God at his baptism, or that his sonship consisted of a moral oneness with God, a relationship of dependence upon God in terms of doing God's will, rather than of a oneness in essence with God. And yet, it is most characteristic of Mark to let such a lofty title as this go undefined, to leave his hearer-reader in the dark as to its actual content until he should observe Jesus further and draw his own conclusions regarding his relation to God. The next question to ask, therefore, is, In Mark's Gospel does Jesus act as we would imagine or expect someone "in the form of God" to act?

Mark's answer is that Jesus, from the very beginning of his ministry, is engaged in a titanic struggle with superhuman powers of evil. The world lies not only in God's hand. It is also an arena in which forces hostile to God hold sway. In this "first" Gospel, the shape which such forces assume is first of all that of "demon possession," according to which "unclean spirits" (note the word "unclean," which is not a medical but a religious term, i.e. the description of a malady which makes life impossible in the religious community) inhabit and tyrannize men. The very first public act which Jesus performs is the driving out or exorcism of an unclean spirit (1:23-28).[3]

By its position, Mark obviously intends to tell us that Jesus' coming denotes some radical change in the balance of power which has till now prevailed in the world. Those superhuman, antigodly powers which till now have been free to work their will have suddenly met their match. Indeed, their prince and leader, Satan, as he was called by writers between the Testaments, was already beaten in that secret wilderness struggle following the baptism (1:12-13), a victory from which the lesser victories of the exorcisms follow logically. Thus the Jesus of Mark "commands" the unclean spirits (1:27), casts them out (1:34, 39; cf. 3:11-12; 9:14-29), destroys them (5:1-20), gives to his disciples, even to strangers untutored by him, authority to cast them out (3:15, 6:13; 9:38-41).

Since Mark knows nothing more of the origins of diseases than his contemporaries, he undoubtedly attributes to demon possession illnesses which modern man would prefer to call mental-physical or psychosomatic. He even suggests that natural diseases are attributable to the same cause. Jesus' cure of the deaf-mute, for example, has more the nature of an exorcism than of medical treatment:

> And taking him aside from the multitude privately, he put his fingers into his ears, and he spat and touched his tongue; and looking up to heaven, he sighed, and said to him, "Ephphatha," that is, "Be opened" (7:33-34).

Such a view as Mark holds may strike us for all the world as primitive and outmoded, but of one thing our "preacher" is convinced—calamity, whether it take the form of demon possession or a withered hand, is not from God. That is, calamity is not willed by God or sent by God. On the contrary, it is a thwarting of God's purpose for man. It is for this reason, primarily, that Mark attributes an unclean spirit or a hemorrhage to the same evil cause, and for this reason Jesus not merely exorcises but also heals—Simon's mother-in-law (1:29-31); those "sick with various diseases" (1:34; cf. 3:10; 6:5, 53-57); the paralytic (2:1-12); the man with the withered hand (3:1-6); the woman with the flow of blood (5:34); the deaf-mute (7:31-37); the blind man of Bethsaida (8:22-26), and Bartimaeus (10:46-52).

But the climax to such activity, of course, is to be seen in Jesus' encounter with death, the last enemy of all. "Talitha cumi!" he shouts to the corpse of the twelve-year-old in chapter 5—"and immediately the girl got up and walked" (5:21-24, 35-42). And on either side of this narrative are set two stories which carry the same message, both of them storm-narratives. In chapter 4, vv. 35-41, treating of Jesus' stilling of wind and sea, and in the narrative of his appearance on the water in chapter 6, vv. 45-52, we encounter no mere feats of magic over against the elements, but rather "parables" in which are announced Jesus' power over death, symbolized by sea and storm. The fact that in Mark the miracles of Jesus are never for the purpose of displaying his power but for the purpose of bringing help, and the fact that these two stories show every indication of having penetrated the text of Mark here from elsewhere, viz., from the resurrection narrative,[4] justify our regarding them as "action parables" in which Jesus' power over death is signalized.

Such acts as these overwhelm his audiences ("What is this? A new teaching! With authority he commands even the unclean spirits, and they obey him," 1:27; "We never saw anything like this!" 2:12; "He has done all things well; he even makes the deaf hear and the dumb speak," 7:37; cf. 6:42), make him the object of a whole city's attention (1:33; cf. 1:45; 3:10; 5:24; 6:53-56), and fill some with fear sufficent to beg him to leave their neighborhood (5:17). Jesus produces amazement in his own disciples ("Who then is this, that even wind and sea obey him?" 4:41) or causes them to cry out, "Why could we not . . . . ?" (9:28). He thus justifies the Baptist's description of him as the "Mightier One" (1:7), the Stronger than the strong who binds the strong man (i.e. Satan) and plunders his house (3:27). In such scenes Mark intends that his hearer should put to himself the question whether or not these cosmic conflicts which inevitably result in Jesus' favor are the kind of thing from which anyone less than a God can walk away the victor!

There is more. If, at the outset, Jesus emerges as the Stronger than the strong, as healer, at the same time he appears as the forgiver. In chapter 2, following his exorcism of the unclean spirit and healing of the leper, Jesus announces forgiveness. One of the most unusual narratives in Mark's "sermon" is the story of Jesus' healing of the paralytic, in which the climax is reached not with the command to take up his bed and go home, but with the startling announcement that his sins are forgiven (2:2-11). If Mark assigns demon possession as well as natural illness to the same cause, in this story he makes an organic connection between illness and sin, hence the word, "My son, your sins are forgiven" (2:5). There is no attempt to explain the word "forgiveness" psychologically, as though the paralytic's malady derived from a particular, specific sin. Like every faithful Jew of his day, Mark knew only that sin and suffering were somehow linked. Again, not that much suffering was the inevitable result of much sin, or that health and prosperity were the natural outcome of much goodness—this kind of Puritan mathematics is nowhere to be found in Mark. Rather, in this narrative, Mark again makes clear that all the ills which afflict man, whether in body or spirit, have their origin in a power or powers intent on opposing the sovereign purpose of God, and that therefore the word which sets them free must not be merely a word to the inner man, but to all of him, to man as a whole. It thus makes little difference whether or not that word is a command to walk, to see, to hear, to rise from the dead, or the announcement of forgiveness. Cleansing, healing, forgiveness are all of a piece. Thus Jesus puts to his critics the question, "Which is easier, to say to the paralytic, 'Your sins are forgiven,' or to say, 'Rise, take up your pallet and walk'?" (2:9).

Much more important for Mark, however, is that such a word should come from the lips of *Jesus;* that with *Jesus* the word of healing or the word of forgiveness should be one and the same word; that *Jesus* should announce to those at table with him that *he* "came not to call the righteous, but sinners" (2:17), that a man's fate and destiny should be conditional upon his attitude toward *him* (3:28-30). This kind of behavior is either a shocking usurpation of the divine prerogative on the part of a megalomaniac, or something else, something incomparably greater and grander. Mark will never come out flat-footedly and announce in stentorian tones what that "something else" is. He is not that kind of preacher. He allows the question to be put by the enemy, and by it hopes to provoke his hearer-reader to ask the question of himself and to supply the proper answer:

> "Why does this man speak thus? It is blasphemy!
> Who can forgive sins but God alone?" (2:7).

Indeed!

There is still more. The Jesus of Mark is gatherer of the community as well as its provider. In chapter 1, Jesus calls to Simon and Andrew, "Follow me." They immediately leave their nets to follow (1:17-18). Modern preachers love to regale their audiences with some kind of psychological preparation for this scene, to tell how Simon and Andrew, yearning for Messiah, must have known of Jesus prior to this encounter, must have seen him at work, heard him preach, and how that calling by the Galilean sea must have been the culmination of months, perhaps years of waiting. But such psychologizing is alien to Mark. Above all, he intends by his portrayal of the disciples' sudden response to paint larger than life the one whose call evokes such quick reply and thus stimulate his hearer to ask himself whether or not this Jesus bears any similarity to that One who in ancient time called, "Let there be light: and there was light" (Gen. 1:3). In each similar scene, Jesus suddenly appears, suddenly calls, and is just as suddenly followed—he says to Levi, " 'Follow me.' And he rose and followed him" (2:14). But Mark's grandest description of Jesus' call by far is contained in vv. 13-14 of chapter 3:

> And he went up into the hills, and called to him those whom he desired; and they came to him. And he appointed twelve, to be with him, and to be sent out . . .

These words contain one of the most massive and suggestive portraits of Jesus given in the Gospel. The area into which Jesus ascends, and which our English versions so feebly translate "the hills," is "the mount" or "mountain range." A casual scanning of the Gospel will reveal that for Mark such references to locale are not merely for the purpose of fixing a scene or event, but carry a weight far beyond the geographical. For example, "Galilee" is not just northern Palestine, west of the Jordan. It is where faith has its home—Jesus comes from Galilee; he begins his preaching there, gains his first disciples and followers there; in Galilee he begins his heathen mission and first proclaims his suffering; in Galilee the disciples first encounter the risen Lord. And the counterfoil of Galilee is Jerusalem, the realm of unbelief, where Jesus meets only opposition and death—Jerusalem, with her magnificent temple and palaces, to be destroyed for her wasted opportunity: "There will not be left here one stone upon another, that will not be thrown down" (13:2).

Accordingly, the "mount" of chapter 3, like all other mounts in the Gospel of Mark (the mount of transfiguration, 9:2; Olivet, site of Jesus' prediction of Jerusalem's ruin and the world's end, 13:3), is a place of disclosure and command, the ruler's throne. From this height Jesus not merely "appoints," as our English Bible so weakly translates, but as the original of Mark has it, *creates* the twelve. The similarity with the first verse of Genesis ("In the beginning God created . . .") cannot be missed—Mark intended it.

The figure of Jesus as dispenser of bread in the story of the Syrophoenician woman;[5] the narrative of the feeding (6:30-44; 8:1-10), the Last Supper scene (14: 22-25) as well as the references to Jesus' table fellowship (cf. 2:15-17; 14:3), while having as their primary point the figure of Messiah at whose banquet many "from east and west" will come to sit (cf. Matt. 8:11; Luke 13:29, a figure which Judaism never furnished with the qualities of God), stir Mark's audience to reminisce upon similar events of Old Testament story. In particular, the dual-account of the feeding (the stories in chapters 6 and 8 are of the same event—in both the disciples find themselves in the same embarrassment; in both Jesus asks the same question), with its references to the confusion (6:34) and hunger of the crowds (8:2-3), to the desert place (8:4), to the number of people fed, as well as its use of "sacred numbers" such as

5, 7, and 3, is highly suggestive of the ancient story in Exodus 16:

> . . . all the congregation of the people of Israel came to the wilderness of Sin, which is between Elim and Sinai . . . . And the whole congregation of the people of Israel murmured against Moses and Aaron in the wilderness, and said to them, "Would that we had died by the hand of the Lord in the land of Egypt, when we sat by the fleshpots and ate bread to the full . . . . Then the Lord said to Moses, "Behold, I will rain bread from heaven for you . . . ." In the evening quails came up and covered the camp; and in the morning dew lay round about the camp. And when the dew had gone up, there was on the face of the wilderness a fine, flake-like thing, fine as hoar-frost on the ground. When the people of Israel saw it, they said to one another, "What is it?" For they did not know what it was. And Moses said to them, "It is the bread which the Lord has given you to eat . . . " (Ex. 16:1-15).

Further, by setting the scene for the "second" feeding in a foreign country ("the region of the Decapolis," 7:31; in Matthew and Luke the feeding occurs in Galilee) Mark turns his narrative into a variant of the story of Elijah and the Gentile widow of Zarephath in I Kings:

> The jar of meal was not spent, neither did the cruse of oil fail, according to the word of the Lord which he spoke by Elijah (1 Kings 17:16).

To complete his variation on the theme as contained in the first line of Paul's "hymn," Jesus is equipped with superhuman knowledge. He knows the questions of his critics before they are asked (2:8) and divines their hypocrisy (12:15). In the press of the crowd he perceives that "power" has gone from him and asks, "Who touched my garments?" (5:30-31). He augurs the beast on which he will ride into Jerusalem (11:2-6) and the room in which he will hold the last meal with his disciples (including the water-carrier who will lead his disciples there, cf. 14:12-16). The person of his betrayer, the disciples' defection at the crucifixion, and Peter's denial are all known to him beforehand (14:17-18, 42; 14:27, 30). In almost every instance, Mark takes care to indicate that what is involved is not mere logical inference but a real omniscience by pointing to the amazement of onlookers or disciples ("his disciples said to him, 'You see the crowd pressing around you, and yet you say, 'Who touched me?' " 5:31), or by adding that events took place just as Jesus had predicted ("And the disciples set out and went to the city, and found it as he had told them; and they prepared the passover," 14:16; cf. 14:43-49, 50, 72).

In light of this heaping up of clues, hints, and inferences which mark the portion of the "sermon" we have just outlined, can there be any doubt that Mark's purpose is to tease his audience to the recognition that the man from Nazareth was "in the form" of that One who declared:

> " 'See now that I, even I am he, and there is no god beside me; I kill and I make alive; I wound and I heal; and there is none that can deliver out of my hand . . . ' " (Deut. 32:39).

Off the Pedestal

> **[He] did not count equality with God a thing to be grasped, but emptied himself, taking the form of a servant, being born in the likeness of men** (Phil. 2:6b-7).

Adjusting his sermon to such a thought, Mark first of all supplies Jesus with all the traits native to mere men. He drives out the spirits, heals, forgives, gathers, feeds, and predicts. Yet he is unable openly to enter a town (1:45), to be hid (7:24). More than this, he is unable to do a "mighty work" in his native city (6:5), as though his acts did not at all depend upon his own power but upon such things as geography and the attitude of his audience. (Matthew simply eliminates the word "unable" from his account, leaving the impression that because of Nazareth's unbelief Jesus refused to do a mighty work there, 13:58.) Jesus, further, puts questions to which he apparently does not know the answer. In the feeding narrative he asks, "How many loaves have you? Go and see" (6:38; cf. 8:5). (Note that in the Fourth Gospel the writer appends to Jesus' query the words, "This he said to test him, for he himself knew what he would do," 6:6, thus erasing any hint of limited knowledge in Jesus.) At times Jesus is not privy to his disciples' conversation and asks, "What are you discussing?" (9:16), "What were you discussing on the way?" (9:33). (Both stories are eliminated in Matthew's and Luke's accounts; cf. Matthew 7:14 ff., 18:1 ff. and Luke 9:37 ff., 46 ff.) Of the time of Jerusalem's ruin and the end of the world he confesses total ignorance: "But of that day or that hour no one knows, not even the angels in heaven, nor the Son . . ." (13:32). And this portrait of Jesus as limited in knowledge and comprehension reaches its awful climax in that cry of dereliction from the cross: "My God, my God, why . . . ?" (15:34).

Though, as we noted, Mark, unlike modern biographers, gives virtually no description of the inner life of his hero, he at times does give a quick look-see into what might be called Jesus' "psychic states," and thus adds to this altogether human picture. Jesus is "grieved" at men's hardness of heart (3:5); he marvels at their unbelief (6:6); he has "compassion" on the hungry crowd (6:34; 8:2); he "sighs deeply in his spirit" when Pharisees seek a sign from him (8:12); he is "indignant" at the disciples' treatment of children (10:14); he betrays his love for the rich man (10:21); he is "greatly distressed and troubled," his soul is "very sorrowful" at Gethsemane (14:33-34).

It is most unusual that Mark, whose initial portrait of Jesus struck us at once as massive, colossal, should, in these scenes at least, place a stress upon his humanity not shared by his co-evangelists, Matthew and Luke. For in almost every instance cited, Matthew, Luke, or both avoid such a glimpse into Jesus' inner life as Mark gives, suggesting that for them such references seemed somehow inappropriate. The reference to Jesus' anger in Mark 3:5 does not appear in Matthew 12:12-13 and Luke 6:10. His awe at his audience's unbelief in 6:6 is absent from Matthew 13:38 and Luke 4:24. Jesus' "compassion" for the hungry is not referred to in Luke's parallel version (Luke 9:11). In Matthew 16:4; 12:39 and Luke 11:29 there is no hint of a "sigh" at the demand for a sign; no impatience at the disciples' treatment of children in Matthew 19:14 and Luke 18:16, and Jesus' "love" for the rich man is not mentioned in Matthew 19:21 and Luke 18:22.

The Jesus of Mark also suffers physical distresses common to all—he is hungry (11:12), he dies, and is buried (15:37, 44, 46-47; 16:6b). In fact, as though for some reason compelled to "nail down" this point for all time, Mark takes particular note of Jesus' rapid death and Pilate's reaction to it:

> And Pilate wondered if he were already dead [not, he wondered whether Jesus were already dead, but, he was amazed that he had so soon expired]; and summoning the centurion, he asked him whether he was already dead. And when he learned from

> the centurion that he was dead, he granted the body to Joseph (Mark 15:44-45; a report which occurs neither in Matthew nor in Luke).

All this is hardly calculated to yield a picture of some "easy living" Olympian Zeus, in unmoved and untroubled repose observing men crawling like ants across the billboard of time.

The second line of Paul's "hymn" has its most vivid illustration, however, in Mark's treatment of Jesus' role as the Servant of God. The voice at the baptism which declares, "Thou art my beloved Son; with thee I am well pleased," at first glance suggests that here Mark is placing Jesus on an equality with God. The reason is simply that with 1900 years of Christian confession behind him, the reader or hearer naturally freights that word "Son" with its customary load—oneness with God in essence. And there is no doubt that Mark gives to Jesus such an exalted place. But as noted above,[6] a title which Mark applies to Jesus in a particular instance may be sufficiently ambiguous to suggest that it is not only Jesus' Godhead or Jesus' equality with God which the evangelist has in mind. The voice at the baptism is a case in point.

First of all, the language or content of the voice is highly reminiscent of a passage in Isaiah:

> Behold my servant, whom I uphold, my chosen, in whom my soul delights; I have put my Spirit upon him, he will bring forth justice to the nations (Isa. 42:1).

In this "Servant Song," as well as in others (cf. Isaiah 53; 61), the prophet is intent primarily on outlining the Servant's *function:*

> He will not cry or lift up his voice, or make it heard in the street; a bruised reed he will not break, and a dimly burning wick he will not quench; he will faithfully bring forth justice. He will not fail or be discouraged till he has established justice in the earth; and the coastlands wait for his law (Isa. 42:2-4).

From such "songs" it is also clear that whatever the Servant does he does not do independently, but only as one who is sent:

> ". . . The Lord has anointed me to bring good tidings to the afflicted; he has sent me to bind up the brokenhearted . . ." (Isa. 61:1).

Indeed, without the Spirit of God, the Servant could not perform his office. Hence Isaiah's stress upon the Servant's equipment with the Spirit of God:

> I have put my Spirit upon him (Isa. 42:1).

> The Spirit of the Lord God is upon me, because the Lord has anointed me to bring good tidings (Isa. 61:1).

And if the prophet should on occasion speak of the Servant as he is in himself, it is the Servant in his solidarity with Israel, not his oneness with God, which is most often emphasized:

> "But now hear, O Jacob my servant, Israel whom I have chosen! . . . Fear not, O Jacob my servant, Jeshurun whom I have chosen . . . " (Isa. 44:1-2).

Beyond its customary interpretation, then, the voice at the Jordan sets up a chain of connection with biblical utterances according to which the Servant is seen first of all as God's agent or instrument, as one who is subordinate to God's will. The voice, together with the description of the Spirit's descent at Jesus' baptism (1:10), makes the similarity between Mark's portrait of Jesus and Isaiah's Servant, Spirit-bearer too striking to be mere happenstance.

This concentration upon Jesus as the Servant furnished with the Spirit of God is a feature of Mark's "sermon" which makes it kin to almost every piece of the New Testament. To cite just a few examples, the echoes of Mark's baptismal account in Matthew, Luke, and John (Matt. 4:17; Luke 3:22; John 1:32-34); the "scriptures" which Jesus expounds on the Emmaus journey (Luke 24:25-27, 32, and the almost literal repetition of these verses in Acts 17:2-3; 26:22-23; cf. also the story of Philip and the Ethiopian in Acts 8:26-39); the references to the "Servant" in the speeches of Acts (3:13, 26; 4:27, 30) and in Paul; the constant emphasis upon the sufferings of Jesus in the First Epistle of Peter (cf. 1 Peter 2:21 ff.), and Second Peter's preoccupation with the baptismal and transfiguration themes, all have as their background the Isaian figure of the "Servant of God."

It is highly probable that in such references as noted above we encounter fragments of the very earliest Christian preaching about Jesus, preaching which originated with the first community of believers in Palestine and which later, though only in part, came to be embedded in such Hellenistic confessions and "hymns" as Paul quotes in Philippians 2. This oldest, "Galilean" setting forth of Jesus as God's Servant could not hold the field alone against the grander and loftier titles applied to Jesus by the church when it transplanted itself from Jewish to Greek and Roman soil. Only now and again does it appear in our New

Testament, like a shard from an ancient ruin. On the other hand, this Servant-motif could not altogether disappear. First of all, because it provided the Christian community with an explanation for the tragedy of Jesus' crucifixion in face of the taunts and jeers of its enemies —"he was wounded for our transgressions, he was bruised for our iniquities; upon him was the chastisement that made us whole, and with his stripes we are healed" (Isa. 53:5). Second, because it reflected Jesus' own understanding of himself and his mission. Hence, though only once, the Jesus of Mark speaks of himself as Servant at the most crucial point of his career—the final journey to Jerusalem:

> ". . . whoever would be great among you must be your servant, and whoever would be first among you must be slave of all. For the Son of man also came not to be served but to serve, and to give his life as a ransom for many" (10:45; cf. also the oblique reference in 9:35, and the witness to "him who sent me" in 9:37).

The one whom Mark describes as "taking the form of a servant" is a Servant without a will of his own. Immediately after narrating the story of Jesus' baptism, Mark describes him as "driven" by the Spirit into the wilderness (1:12). In George Stevens' film production "The Greatest Story Ever Told," following his baptism Jesus clambers up the mountainside to encounter his tempter. Aside from the curious "twist" which the director gives this scene—Satan sits in a cave eating his lunch, dressed like a character out of Steinbeck's *Grapes of Wrath*—the impression conveyed to the viewer is that this encounter is foreseen, if not actually planned, by Jesus. Fulton Oursler's volume on which the film is largely based is much less cautious in its description of Jesus' exercise of initiative:

> On a hillside He found a cavern and there He made His solitary camp. His sole reason for retreating to this grotto was that He must become acquainted with human suffering and temptation. He had to know them at first-hand and altogether before He could begin His work. . . . He must overcome temptation Himself—as a man, not as God—before He advised other men what they must do. That was why Jesus made His way into this gigantesque waterless region . . . .[7]

But the Jesus of Mark is "flung out into the wilderness." Under the propulsion of the Spirit of God he possesses little more self-reliance or self-determination than the unclean spirits whom he "drives out" (in the original Greek of Mark, the same verb is used in both instances) and forbids to speak. In this scene, at any rate, that colossal figure which stills storm and sea has left his pedestal and become the instrument of God, possessed by the divine Spirit as if without regard to his own identity, like Balaam, bribed to curse Israel but unable to utter anything but a blessing because "the Lord put a word in [his] mouth" (Numbers 23:5).

Mark further casts Jesus in his Servant role by describing him as one whose power is derived. In the synagogue at Capernaum the crowd is amazed at Jesus' teaching, "for he taught them as one who had authority, and not as the scribes" (1:22). The accent in this little verse falls on that word "authority." To be sure, there were external differences between Jesus' and the scribes' teaching. The scribe could scarcely open his mouth without citing precedent in support of his opinion. His teaching inevitably included a "Rabbi so-and-so said that Rabbi so-and-so said that Rabbi so-and-so said, etc." until every expert on the question had been rung into the bargain. For the scribe, precedent was needed to nail down the argument. When Jesus mounted the pulpit, he spoke out without marshaling the evidence of hoary antiquity to support him. Such behavior was bound to strike his hearer as novel and revolutionary. But it was not these purely formal aspects which awakened such a response from Jesus' audience. The crowd instinctively felt that Jesus had "authority" —his own or someone else's perhaps made little difference—power to lay the Scriptures bare in a strange and inviting way. Mark in turn sees clearly what the crowd only intuited, that the freshness and vitality of Jesus' teaching lay not in any formal difference between his teaching and that of the scribes, not even in Jesus' own genius, but in that Other in whose name he spoke. In other words, for Mark there is no authority which is not derived, no power which Jesus possesses which is not given him. He is a Servant.

In that same Capernaum scene Jesus astonishes the crowds with his exorcisms. No doubt, the fact that Jesus cast out demons produced astonishment. But Jesus was neither the first nor the last to accomplish such feats. Palestine, the whole Mediterranean world, was a-swarm with "physicians" who healed successfully. What ultimately amazed his audience was that he taught with an "authority" which was reflected in his exorcisms.[8] And, with that word "authority" Mark again gives the story a turn which compels us to look beyond Jesus to Another.

In chapter 2 of Mark, Jesus announces forgiveness to the paralytic. The natural reaction of the crowd is that he puts himself on an equality with God. And indeed, by telling the story Mark intends to prod his hearer to acknowledge that equality. But in the very next moment it is an entirely different figure which emerges, one without independence, a figure empty of self, who forgives "on commission"—"But that you may know that the Son of man has authority on earth to forgive sins . . . " (2:10)—the Servant of God.

If Jesus speaks of himself only once as servant (10:45), a score of times he points away from himself to Another. He speaks of the One who sent him (9:37); he acknowledges to the ambitious sons of Zebedee that it is not in his power to grant a seat at his right or left hand (10:40); he announces that the Father in heaven has the ultimate right to forgive (11:25), that it is he who is sovereign over time and events, who cuts short the period of evil's reign (13:20), he who alone knows the day and the hour of the coming of the Son of man to judgment (13:32).

But all these utterances turn pale before Jesus' astonishing words to the rich young ruler:

> And as he was setting out on his journey, a man ran up and knelt before him, and asked him, "Good Teacher, what must I do to inherit eternal life?" And Jesus said to him, "Why do you call me good? No one is good but God alone. You know the commandments . . . " (10:17-19a).

For Matthew, these words were too jarring, too liable to misinterpretation to be repeated. Accordingly, the second evangelist altered them to read:

> And behold, one came up to him, saying, "Teacher, what good deed must I do, to have eternal life?" And he said to him, "Why do you ask me about what is good? One there is who is good. If you would enter life, keep the commandments" (Matt. 19:16-17).

Not only Matthew boggled at Jesus' disclaimer of goodness. These words have proved a source of embarrassment for a host of interpreters since Matthew's day. One scholar writes that Jesus refused the title "Good Teacher" because his and the young man's conceptions of goodness were as different as night and day. Another states that Jesus refused the title because the young man's question concealed his disobedience toward God; still another writes that Jesus would have none of the conventional flattery. Good old Father Martin himself attempts to squeeze out of the difficulty:

> But the Lord will not allow the word Good, for the Pharisee (!) does not apply it to God. This is the first mistake he makes, that he views Christ as a mere man and wishes to apply the term "good" to him. Then [the Lord] is quickly offended and will not be flattered, and this sounds as though Christ would deny that he is God, for he will not be called good, will not have the title he deserves.[9]

Now if Mark had intended to fix the cause of Jesus' disclaimer in the young man's attitude, in his distorted idea of goodness, in his disobedience, his desire to flatter, or in his inability to see Jesus as he truly was, he would have done so clearly and unambiguously. He would have appended a note, just as he does in the scene of Jesus' encounter with his enemies in chapter 2—"And immediately Jesus, perceiving in his spirit that they thus questioned among themselves, etc." As Mark records it, there is not one hint of insincerity in the young man's question. On the contrary, despite his inability to "come, follow," Mark writes that Jesus loved him! (10:21). (Have Matthew and Luke expunged this item from the record to make it easier, perhaps, to attribute an inferior motive to the rich man's question?) This is hardly the kind of treatment which Pharisees and flatterers receive elsewhere in the Gospel.

The words must stand as they are. And as they are they mean simply what they say—God alone is good. Everything good comes from God, belongs to God alone. Even the goodness of Jesus. If Mark takes the thought of the first line of the Christ-hymn ("being in the form of God") so seriously that he is in danger of portraying an unearthly Christ, he takes the thought of the second ("emptied himself, taking the form of a servant") with an equal seriousness and runs the risk of reducing Jesus to a mere man. But even the Fourth Gospel, which is far less concerned with the humanity of Jesus than the other three, records such startling statements as these:

> "I can do nothing on my own authority; as I hear I judge . . . " (John 5:30).
>
> " . . . I have come in my Father's name . . . " (John 5:43).
>
> " . . . I have come down from heaven, not to do my own will, but the will of him who sent me . . . " (John 6:38).
>
> "My teaching is not mine, but his who sent me . . . " (7:16).
>
> " . . . I do not seek my own glory; there is One who seeks it and he will be the judge . . . " (8:50).

Crucified

And being found in human form he humbled himself and became obedient unto death, even death on a cross (Phil. 2:8).

As noted above,[10] when Mark's sermon approaches the theme contained in this line from Paul's hymn, it takes on a concern for detail and sequence which is evident nowhere else in the Gospel. Till now tying his outline together with such little connectors as "and," "as," "again," etc., in chapters 14 and 15 Mark suddenly waxes scrupulous in the matter of detail, heaping upon his hearer-reader a cluster of precise data dealing with Jesus' arrest, trial and crucifixion:

> . . . two days before the Passover . . . (14:1).
> "Not during the feast . . . " (14:2).
> On the first day of Unleavened Bread . . . (14:12).
> When it was evening . . . (14:17).
> " . . . this very night, before the cock crows twice . . . " (14:30).
> As soon as it was morning . . . (15:1).
> It was the third hour . . . (15:25).
> And when the sixth hour had come, there was darkness over the whole land until the ninth hour (15:33).
> At the ninth hour . . . (15:34).
> And when evening had come . . . (15:42).

There can be little doubt—the preacher is warming to his climax. What has preceded has been by way of introduction. Details of time and place, previously dealt with in an off-hand manner, suddenly take on significance as so many peals of a bell calculated to alert the listener and toll the events unforgettably into his brain. So far, parables, deeds, miracles, conflict-speeches have been lumped together with little care for their temporal order. It was necessary merely to show their logical relationship. But now that we are at the heart of the matter, everything must be told with exactitude.

There is another striking feature in this part of Mark's sermon. The very style is made to fit the theme. The words "humbled" and "obedient" suggest a relinquishing of the reins, submission to Another's will. If there looms behind those words in Paul's hymn that figure of the Servant whom Isaiah describes almost exclusively in the passive voice—"*was* despised and rejected . . . *was* wounded . . . *was* bruised . . . *was* oppressed . . . *was* taken away . . . *was* cut off out of the land of the living . . . *was* numbered with the transgressors, etc." (Isaiah 53)—the same figure, earlier in the Gospel placed alongside or merged with the figure of the Colossus, now crowds everything and everyone else off the stage. The Jesus of Mark 14 and 15 is no longer master of his destiny.

Compare, for a moment, the abrupt change of style in these two chapters with what precedes. Chapter 2 begins, "And when [Jesus] returned to Capernaum"; chapter 3, "Again he entered the synagogue"; chapter 4, "And he began to teach"; chapter 5, "And when he had come out of the boat"; 6, "He went away from there and came to his own country"; 8, "He called his disciples to him"; 9, "And he said to them"; chapter 10, "And he left there and went to the region of Judea"; chapter 11, "And when they drew near to Jerusalem . . . he sent two of his disciples"; 12, "And he began to speak to them in parables"; 13, "And as he came out of the temple . . . ." In every instance, Jesus "has the action." But in 14 and 15 others—the woman with the alabaster jar of ointment, Judas Iscariot, the disciples, Peter, the high priest, witnesses, guards, Pilate, Simon of Cyrene, two robbers, Joseph of Arimathea, the Maries, and Salome—everyone else under the sun but Jesus is subject of the verb! Jesus is not caught by stealth. He knows what is ahead for him and in this sense retains a certain sovereignty over what takes place. He announces, e.g., that the woman with the jar has anointed him for burial (14:8); he miraculously arranges his last meeting-place with his disciples (14:12-16); he predicts the treachery of Judas (14:18, 42), the defection of the disciples (14:27), and Peter's denial (14:30). But he makes no move to forestall what he knows. With one exception, he allows himself to be borne aloft on the stream of events. With anyone else, to be forewarned is to be forearmed. Not with Jesus—his action is inaction. The scene before the high priest, or before Pilate, best characterizes his role:

> And the high priest stood up in the midst, and asked Jesus, "Have you no answer to make? What is it that these men testify against you?" But he was silent and made no answer (14:60-61)

> And Pilate again asked him, "Have you no answer to make? See how many charges they bring against you." But Jesus made no further answer, so that Pilate wondered (15:4-5).

The contrast between this Jesus and the Jesus of the Fourth Gospel who frightens his captors (John 18:4-6); puts his judges on trial (18:19-23); announces to Pilate that he is but a tool of a power from above (19:10-11); welds together a family from his cross (19:25-27), in short, who turns his gibbet into a "victor's car," is as great as the difference between heaven and earth.

Even in Matthew, Jesus is infinitely more regal, more "in command" than in Mark. In the garden, when his defender unsheathes his sword he roars:

> "Do you think that I cannot appeal to my Father, and he will at once send me more than twelve legions of angels?" (Matt. 26:53).

And his death is the signal for a catastrophe of nature:

> And behold, the curtain of the temple was torn in two, from top to bottom; and the earth shook, and the rocks were split; the tombs also were opened, and many bodies of the saints who had fallen asleep were raised . . . (Matt. 27:51-52).

In Luke, Jesus assumes every bit as majestic a role. He orders his followers to procure weapons, that the scriptures might be fulfilled (Luke 22:36-37); he preaches to the weeping women along the Via Dolorosa (23:28-31); he opens Paradise to the dying thief (23:39-43), and above all, announces that his enemies would be powerless if he had not been handed them, as if on a platter:

> "When I was with you day after day in the temple, you did not lay hands on me. But this is your hour, and the power of darkness" (Luke 22:53).

In Mark's account of the Passion, Jesus' passivity is unrelieved.

But if the Jesus of Mark goes to his death without lifting a finger, that nonaction is not the sort which afflicts men who have been caught in the "fell clutch of circumstance" and cannot change what is to be. True, from the very outset a necessity lay on Jesus, a necessity he acknowledged more than once:

> . . . the Son of man must suffer (8:31).
> "For the Son of man goes as it is written of him . . . " (14:21).

And, what one writer says of that little word "must" in Luke's Gospel, viz., that Jesus viewed his career and its outcome, his entire existence as prisoner to that necessity,[11] applies equally to Mark. But it was not as though he had no other alternative. On the contrary, our preacher makes crystal-clear that Jesus' being swept along on the crest of things was the result of his own prior decision, the decision to make that "must," that necessity, his own. That decision was made, ultimately, beyond the brook Kidron at the foot of Olives—in Gethsemane.

Describing the scene, Mark first states that Jesus abandoned the majority of his followers. Only three—Peter, James, and John—accompanied him, the same who witnessed his transfiguration (9:2-8). Jesus' words in 14:34—"my soul is very sorrowful"—are a quotation from the Psalms (42:6, 12; 43:5). The Psalmist uttered them in prayer to God. Jesus, however, addresses them to the three and adds the phrase "unto death." Is death, perhaps, the friend which can free him from his unbearable agony? For the three, at any rate, the riddle of this agony is not solved. They merely receive the command to "remain here, and watch." Watch for what? For danger? The word is given in view of what they are about to hear.

Jesus goes deeper into the garden. The High Priest ascends the Holy of Holies alone. His companions remain before the curtain. This is the hour and this the place of that service which is required of him! Jesus falls to the earth, forehead and knee touching the ground. He prays. Mark gives first the substance of his prayer (v. 35), then the direct quote, as though the hearer had first to be prepared before the sacred words themselves could be given. Why should this "hour" pass? So far, the reason is dark and obscure.

The prayer of Jesus opens with a bilingual address common to the later Gentile community — "Abba, Father" (v. 36; cf. Rom. 8:15). The prayer continues with an invocation of the power of God—"all things are possible to thee" (v. 36a). This power is able to avert not only what is humanly inescapable, but even what is inescapable from the point of view of God. Then Jesus pleads, "Remove this cup from me!" Whose cup? The "hour" is God's, and the "cup" is God's. So it is not dark fate which hangs over him. This "cup" is the unspeakable burden which God gives to him and only to him! Silence all around. Then the words, "Yet not what I will, but what thou wilt." Nowhere else in all the Gospel is the will of God set over against another's so directly and immediately. Jesus, who more than any other can claim a peculiar right to speak of his own will, bows himself to one higher.

With infinite simplicity Mark now contrasts the figures of the praying Jesus, torn with grief and anxiety, and the sleeping disciples:

> "Simon, are you asleep? Could you not watch one hour? Watch and pray . . . " (vv. 37-38a).

The "hour" is imminent, the "hour" in which the dark powers will once more seize control, when the faithful must suffer and wait the daybreak with trembling, the "hour" which renders watching a duty and sleeping a desertion. If Jesus' earlier words sounded reveille, his word in v. 38b blows taps—"the spirit is willing, but the flesh is weak." This may be the "hour," and the human "spirit" may recognize its requirement, but man is a divided creature whose "flesh" is too weak to be borne aloft!

Mark records the scene, twice, three times. Jesus' prayer fades; the sleep into which the disciples have fallen looms up. Mark says that when Jesus came to them the second time and found them sleeping, "they did not know what to answer him" (v. 40). As though their sleep were an alien power which had overwhelmed them. Only Jesus' final word rouses them.

In all of this there is no voice from heaven. Between Jesus' prayer and his summons, "Rise, let us be going" (v. 42), the only sound to be heard is the disciples' snoring. Luke, possibly to assure the Christians in his care that God was not deaf to Jesus' agony, adds the words:

> And there appeared to him an angel from heaven, strengthening him (Luke 22:43).

But if it is legitimate to see some kind of connection between the disciples' sleeping and the content of Jesus' prayer—three times he turns back to the three, after praying an equal number of times (vv. 37, 40, 41) —then it is in that sleep that Jesus reads the answer to his prayer. God has refused him his petition. The "hour" will not pass by. He must empty the cup and empty it alone. As one writer puts it:

> The sleep of the disciples, token of human faithlessness and sinful weakness, is also the enigmatically veiled and yet manifest answer of God to the prayer of the Son of Man.[12]

A thousand times men have drawn comparisons between this decision of Jesus and that of Socrates, made a good four hundred years before. Accused of being an evil-doer and corruptor of Athens' youth, of rejecting state divinities and introducing new gods, Socrates was condemned to death. His aged friend Crito appeared at his prison cell and urged him to escape:

> "Fear not. There are persons who at no great cost are willing to save you and bring you out of prison . . . do not . . . hesitate about making your escape, and do not say, as you did in the court, that you will have a difficulty in knowing what to do with yourself if you escape. For men will love you in other places to which you may go, and not in Athens only. . . Nor can I think that you are justified, Socrates, in betraying your own life when you might be saved . . . "[13]

Socrates, refusing, replied:

"Let me follow the intimations of the will of God."[13]

Like Socrates, the Jesus of Gethsemane is not the pawn of an ineluctable fate, but one who has a will of his own, to surrender which is all his own! For if God's Servant had no option but to drink the cup, where would the humbling, where would the obedience be?

Tersely, in a few brief sentences, Mark describes the outcome of Jesus' "obedience unto death." He was crucified between two thieves, refused opiates of any kind, and died within six hours.

The world has witnessed more horrible deaths than the death of Jesus. Our minds are still reeling with pictures of Congo tribesmen, with the expertise of trained surgeons disemboweling their enemies and forcing them to chew their own entrails. In itself the death of Jesus has met its match a thousand times over. It is only when Mark's hearer reflects upon that death in its historical context and, finally, ponders that death within the context of what Mark has had to say till now, that it takes on such awful significance.

To begin with, the Jew had a horror of crucifixion. Not merely because it was a painful way to die. And it was painful to hang there with one's limbs outstretched, body baking in the sun and every pore crying out with thirst.[14] The combination of such bodily torture with the desperate frustration of being robbed from dying modestly, of hanging naked and exposed to public gaze, made crucifixion an unbearable prospect. In Jesus' day it had become the ignominious death par excellence. But it was not so much this the Jew feared as the fact that to die on a cross meant, first of all, to be defiled by heathen hands. Crucifixion was an exclusively pagan torture which Rome inherited from the

Orient through its wars with Carthage. The victim could not be buried according to Jewish law—

> " . . . if a man has committed a crime punishable by death and he is put to death, and you hang him on a tree, his body shall not remain all night upon the tree, but you shall bury him the same day . . . " (Deut. 21:22-23a).

He had to hang for days, perhaps even for weeks, while the vultures picked at his flesh. Second, for the Jew crucifixion denoted rejection, expulsion from the community and covenant of God, for only blasphemers and idolators were worthy of such a death. A tractate of the Mishna, the basic portion of the Jewish Talmud, gives the following appraisal:

> The Sages say: None is hanged save the blasphemer and the idolator. . . . How did they hang a man? They put a beam into the ground and a piece of wood jutted from it. The two hands [of the body] were brought together and [in this fashion] it was hanged. R. Jose says: The beam was made to lean against a wall and one hanged the corpse thereon as the butchers do. And they let it down at once; if it remained there overnight a negative command is thereby transgressed, for it is written, *His body shall not remain all night upon the tree, but thou shalt surely bury him the same day; for he that is hanged is a curse against God* (Deuteronomy 21:23); as if to say: Why was this one hanged? Because he blessed (*i.e.* cursed) the Name, and the Name of Heaven was found profaned.[15]

There is no doubt—however loosely or rigorously the Roman government may have stood to his trial and crucifixion—the Jesus of Mark, and of Matthew and Luke for that matter, died a death which his enemies regarded as appropriate to an idolator and blasphemer:

> And those who passed by derided him, wagging their heads, and saying, "Aha! You who would destroy the temple and build it in three days, save yourself, and come down from the cross!" So also the chief priests mocked him to one another with the scribes, saying, "He saved others; he cannot save himself. Let the Christ, the King of Israel, come down now from the cross, that we may see and believe." Those who were crucified with him also reviled him (Mark 15:29-32; cf. Matt. 27:39-44; Luke 23:35-37, 39).

Beyond the pain and agony which such a death involved for one single man, beyond the gross injustice which such an execution involved provided that man were innocent, the death of Jesus has an infinitely darker and more bitter hue against those blinding colors in which Mark earlier portrayed him. The picture would scarcely be any lighter if Mark had contented himself simply with the figure of the Servant; if he had not supplied it with all those suggestions of deity. For whether Jewry ever recognized that God's Anointed should come to die will remain a subject of debate until the end of time. Wherever such an idea may have taken root, it did not represent the majority opinion, and was all but extinct in Jesus' day.

It is hard to see anything but darkness in Mark, chapter 15. The rays of light Matthew allows, with telling of Judas' remorse (27:4); Pilate's intuition of Jesus' innocence (27:18) and his wife's dream (27:19); the catastrophe following his death (27:51-54) and the awe of the crowds; especially the authorities' haunting recollection of Jesus' word that he would rise, and the sealing of the tomb (27:62-66), are all absent from Mark. The light Luke lets in by recording Pilate's desire to release Jesus (23:20-22); Jesus' spurning the women's tears (23:28-31); his three words from the cross (23:34,

43, 46) and the multitudes' awe at the sight (23:48), all of which, calculated or not, assures the reader that Jesus is somehow still in command, appears nowhere in Mark.

And yet, with all this darkness, his Colossus crashing down like that mighty image in the vision of Daniel, it is Mark's conviction that what is happening is not just one more tragedy to be added to the nexus of history but a direct act of God. That conviction is not baldly declared, as in Matthew, "Then was fulfilled what had been spoken by the prophet, etc." (cf. 27:9-10). Characteristically, Mark makes his point by indirection, this time by his style and even by his choice of words.

Mark opens his crucifixion narrative with the announcement that Jesus was "delivered" to Pilate (15:1). Ten times in the chapters preceding, Mark used this term of Jesus (3:19; 9:31; 10:33; 14:10, 11, 18, 21, 41, 42, 44). Why this continual repetition if our preacher does not intend to prod us to a recollection of its appearance in the Servant songs? In Mark's Greek Old Testament, the Bible of the primitive church, Isaiah 53:6 reads: "The Lord *delivered* him for our sins." Again, is not the mention of Jesus' silence before Pilate calculated to conjure up a reminiscence of such words as these:

> Those who seek my life lay their snares, those who seek my hurt speak of ruin, and meditate treachery all the day long. But I am like a deaf man, I do not hear, like a dumb man who does not open his mouth. Yea, I am like a man who does not hear, and in whose mouth are no rebukes (Ps. 38:12-14)?

Or these:

> He was oppressed, and he was afflicted, yet he opened not his mouth; like a lamb that is led to

> the slaughter, and like a sheep that before its shearers is dumb, so he opened not his mouth (Isa. 53:7)?

Can the similarity between Mark's description of the soldiers' mockery in 15:16-20 and the Servant's giving his back to the smiters, his cheeks to those who pulled out the beard, his face to shame and spitting (Isa. 50:6 f.; cf. Isa. 53:3, 5) be mere coincidence? In v. 23, Mark states that they offered Jesus wine mingled with myrrh. Is there perhaps a proverb lurking in the background?

> Give strong drink to him who is perishing, and wine to those in bitter distress; let them drink and forget their poverty, and remember their misery no more (Prov. 31:6-7).

Mark continues that the soldiers divided Jesus' garments and cast lots for them. Any hearer-reader acquainted with the Old Testament could not but recall these words:

> They divide my garments among them, and for my raiment they cast lots (Ps. 22:18)

Of Isaiah's Servant it is written that he was "numbered with the transgressors" (Isa. 53:12), and Mark records that with Jesus "they crucified two robbers, one on his right and one on his left" (15:27). The Greek translations of Lamentations 2:15—"they hiss and wag their heads," and Psalm 22:7—"they make mouths at me, they wag their heads"; of Psalm 22:6—"scorned by men, and despised by the people," Psalm 69:9—"the insults of those who insult thee have fallen on me," and of Psalm 109:25—"I am an object of scorn to my accusers," contain the same verbs as appear in Mark 15:29: "those who passed by derided him, *wagging their heads,*" and in 15:32: "those who were crucified with him also *reviled* him." Jesus' cry of dereliction is almost a word-for-word repetition of Psalm 22:1. The sponge filled with vinegar in 15:36 has its precedent in Psalm 69:21: "and for my thirst they gave me vinegar to drink." Perhaps Mark even intends his audience to hear behind Jesus' last and final shout (15:37) such a word as Psalm 31:22, "Thou didst hear my supplications . . ." (cf. Psalm 39:12). Small wonder Irenaeus described Mark's Gospel as accenting the spirit of prophecy![16]

It cannot be determined with real certainty that the ancient passages just quoted were precisely what Mark had in mind, though the parallelisms between e.g., Psalm 22 and Mark's passion are so numerous as to suggest that the Psalm provided Mark with his outline. A few students of the Gospel have even hazarded the opinion that Psalms such as 22, 69, and Isaiah 53 may together have constituted the earliest Passion story, later to be replaced by the Gospel narratives themselves.

The point in all this, however, is not that Judaism interpreted these Old Testament words of the Messiah. Those "songs" and Psalms which Jesus with sovereign will applied to himself and in which the Christian community, lo, these 1900 years has seen his death prefigured, furnish little proof to the man who has not already believed that this one who was crucified was the "Lord of glory." But the coincidences just noted make amply clear that *for our preacher everything takes place as planned*—"according to the definite plan and foreknowledge of God" (Acts 2:23).

We turn back, for a moment, to the transfiguration narrative of chapter 9. In this scene Jesus takes with him Peter, James, and John, the same three who later accompany him to Gethsemane (9:2; cf. 14:33). Again, what is about to occur is intended only for the eyes of a few. And as if to add further uniqueness to the event, Mark continues that the three are led to a "high mountain." Just as in the story of the calling of the twelve (3:13-14; cf. p. 30) the reference is less for geographical than for theological purposes: what is to take place is a revelation. And, just as at the baptism, the transfiguration has for its essential content a vision and a voice—Jesus appears in a form previously unknown while above him sounds the word, "This is my beloved Son" (9:2-3, 7).

The resemblances between this story and the resurrection accounts cannot be denied. For example, there is close attention to time, an attention paid elsewhere only in connection with the Passion and the resurrection (9:2: "And after six days"—suggestive of the interval between his death and appearance in Galilee). The place of the transfiguration is reminiscent of Jesus' post-resurrection appearance in Matthew 28:16:

> Now the eleven disciples went to Galilee, to the mountain to which Jesus had directed them.

Luke introduces the motif of the sleeping disciples, a feature of the Gethsemane scene, into the transfiguration story, and thus associates Mark 9:2 ff. with 14:32 ff. (cf. Luke 9:32). Jesus' dazzling apparel corresponds to that worn by the heralds of the resurrection (cf. Mark 16:5; Luke 24:4; Matt. 28:3) or by the Judge in Revelation 1:13-14. Moses and Elijah appear in such a way as the Old Testament apocrypha describes those "who from their birth have not tasted death" (II Esdras 6:26). The presence of Peter suggests Paul's word about Jesus' first appearance to that disciple in 1 Corinthians 15:5. The disciples' fright is reminiscent of identical reactions to the resurrection in Mark 16:8, Luke 24:4-5, 36-37, and Matt. 28:4, 8, etc. Accordingly, some have suggested that Mark's transfiguration story is actually a misplaced version of the resurrection.

Yet, while it is true that in this scene Jesus appears as the one he is soon to be, and the transfiguration is thus illumined by an Easter light, three factors, at least, suggest that our preacher intends to put the stress on quite another truth. First of all, the story itself is set at the midpoint of Jesus' three Passion predictions. It follows the prediction of 8:31, is actually of a piece with the prediction in 9:9 ff., and precedes that of 10:32 ff. Secondly, the voice announcing, "This is my beloved Son," clearly connects the "prophet" for whom Moses waited (note the similarity between the command to "listen to him" in Mark 9:7 and the words in Deuteronomy 18:15) with the suffering Servant of Isaiah 42. Finally, the appearance of Elijah (v. 4), the disciples' traditionally Jewish question concerning Elijah's role in the coming age (v. 11), together with Jesus' reply that Elijah has already appeared (in the person of the Baptist) *and has also suffered death* (vv. 12-13), indicate that whatever may have been the original setting of the transfiguration narrative, Mark's intent is to connect it with the motif of Jesus' Passion. On the transfiguration mount, the "prophet" of Moses, the one who "comes after" Elijah-John, is revealed as marked for death by God himself!

For Mark, then, that cry of Jesus from his cross—"My God, my God, why hast thou forsaken me?"[17]—is not merely a wail of surprise at having thrown himself on the wheel of the world only to find himself crushed by it. With that cry Jesus swings himself up to the brassy heaven, pounds on its doors, and demands entry. Hanging suspended between heaven and earth on that tree he is farthest from God and yet nearest to him. For will not the One who willed all this, the One for whom he "humbled himself and became obedient unto death" deliver him? Will not the end of all this be that:

> He has not despised or abhorred the affliction of the afflicted; and he has not hid his face from him, but has heard, when he cried to him (Ps. 22:24)?

On the Pedestal Again

> **Therefore God has highly exalted him and bestowed on him the name which is above every name, that at the name of Jesus every knee should bow, in heaven and on earth and under the earth, and every tongue confess that Jesus Christ is Lord, to the glory of God the Father** (Phil. 2:9-11).

Mark's "sermon" would scarcely have been complete without an account of Jesus' final victory over death, without the announcement that the God who had afflicted his Servant "heard, when he cried to him" (Ps. 22:24). And yet, the brevity of Mark's resurrection story has baffled Christians for a thousand years.

An examination of the 16th chapter of Mark reveals that of the twenty verses normally included in this chapter, only eight have any real claim to genuineness.[18] Verses 9-20—the so-called "Aristion ending"[19]—have no real support in the manuscript evidence or in the testimony of the early church. These verses are so obviously a patchwork of scenes from Luke's and Matthew's accounts that we may confidently assign them to a period in which Mark had been long since dead (i.e., to the middle of the second century). The form and content of the addition to verse 8, which first appears in fifth-century manuscripts of the New Testament, betray its character as a later attempt at supplementation. A third insertion, not included in the

RSV and which records Jesus' reproach of the disciples' unbelief, is from the late fourth or fifth century—the "Freer logion," named for Charles L. Freer of Detroit who acquired it in Egypt in 1906. Eight verses in all, then, are devoted to the theme of Jesus' exaltation, against fifty verses in Luke and twenty in Matthew!

Did Mark, perhaps, compose a longer ending which for some reason has been lost to us? Was that ending inadvertently torn from the Gospel by some careless ancient church archivist? Was it intentionally removed because of its lack of harmony with the stories in the two later rival Gospels which finally came to supersede it in favor and use? Did Mark intend a two-volume work, such as Luke-Acts, only to be interrupted by martyrdom or death by natural causes? Or are the eight verses we possess all that Mark envisioned in the way of a variation on the theme in line four of Paul's "hymn"? Explanations for the abruptness of Mark's conclusion are many and varied, and by choosing whichever explanation suits his fancy, the reader will not have cut himself off from the world of scholars for whom the exercise of intuition or creative imagination in such cases is the only means open to him. For my part, the beginning of a solution was given years ago:

> . . . the first Evangelist's attempt dare not be measured against the more advanced pieces of Matthew and Luke. Mark knows the Risen Lord has appeared and alludes to it in 16:7. Must he tell the story? Does not this indirect note suit a Gospel which has been appropriately described as a Gospel of the "secret epiphanies"? Must the evangelist who pays so little attention to Jesus' words and to the story of his birth and childhood report appearances which go beyond his earthly life, as though he shared our idea of completeness?[20]

In connection with his treatment of the theme in line one of the Christ-hymn we called attention to Mark's habit of making his point by indirection. Jesus' titles are undefined. It is left to the reader to supply them with their proper content. Mark's description of the reaction of friends and enemies to Jesus' activity is calculated to evoke a similar yet profounder response on the part of his hearer-reader. But Mark's resurrection narrative is the ultimate in indirection! Three women approach the tomb for the purpose of anointing the body of Jesus. Worried about the stone sealing the tomb's door, they discover to their surprise that it has been rolled back. Inside the tomb they spy a "young man" who announces Jesus' resurrection and appearance in Galilee. The women flee the tomb and report nothing to anyone. Period! Nothing is said of Jesus' encounter with his disciples (Matt. 28:9 f.; Luke 24:13 ff.), of his charge to evangelize (Matt. 28:18 ff.; Luke 24:44 ff.); nothing of a Galilean supper at which the risen Lord demonstrates his corporeality (Luke 24:36 ff.), nothing of the disciples' joy (Luke 24:52-53).

Add to the extreme brevity of Mark's account its lack of harmony with the resurrection stories in Matthew and Luke, and the problem is merely compounded. For example, in Mark's account, Mary Magdalene, Mary the mother of Jesus, and Salome proceed to the tomb. In Matthew's, Mary Magdalene and the other Mary make the journey. In Luke, Mary Magdalene, Joanna, Mary the mother of James, and other women are mentioned. No reference is made in Matthew's Gospel of the women's purchase of spices. In that same Gospel, the grave is not yet opened when the women appear; in Luke, as in Mark, the stone is already rolled away. The "young man" of Mark who announces the Lord's rising is exchanged for one or two angelic beings in Matthew and

Luke. In contrast to Mark and Luke who give no hint of Jesus' appearance to the women, for Matthew such an appearance clearly antedates any manifestations to the twelve. Further, as if in contradiction to Mark's description of their silence, both Matthew and Luke report that the women informed the disciple community of Jesus' resurrection. And finally, though in Mark Jesus appears, or more precisely, is announced as about to appear to his own in Galilee, in Matthew Jesus appears in Jerusalem as well as in Galilee, but in Luke only in Jerusalem and environs.

To attack each of these discrepancies within the Gospel resurrection narratives would carry us beyond the purpose of our study. At the same time, however, it is important to note that in the majority of instances where Matthew and Luke differ from Mark in their accounts, the reason for the difference lies principally in the area of apologetics. That is, Matthew and Luke write at a moment when the church's opponents have refined their arguments against the resurrection gospel. At Mark's writing, those arguments did not yet require the type of answer or refutation which is implicit in every line of the later two Gospels. To cite just an example or two, Mark evidently feels no necessity for linking up the story of the empty tomb with that of Jesus' appearance in Galilee. These two accounts are so lacking in connection that one 19th century scholar suggests Mark was actually embarrassed by the empty-tomb narrative, but nevertheless felt compelled to add it because he found it alive in church tradition. What is incidental and detached in Mark has become integral in Matthew and Luke. Indeed, for them the empty-tomb sequence provides the motivation for the entire account of Jesus' appearances. For if the women had not reported what they saw and heard, how should the disciples have known where to encounter him? Luke, in obvious reference to earlier tradition, describes the disciples as balking at the women's report—"these words seemed to them an idle tale, and they did not believe them," 24:11 —but later depicts Jesus as wrathful at the disciples' unbelief as related to him by the two companions on the Emmaus road:

> " . . . Some women of our company amazed us. They were at the tomb early in the morning and did not find his body . . . . Some of those who were with us went to the tomb, and found it just as the women had said; but him they did not see. And he said to them, 'O foolish men, and slow of heart to believe . . . ' " (Luke 24:22 ff.),

thus finally giving support to the empty-tomb narrative with the words of Jesus himself. It is highly probable that this connection which Matthew and Luke establish between the account of Jesus' appearances and the empty-tomb story is for the purpose of refuting Jewish or pagan arguments which suggested that the corpse of Jesus was not resuscitated, that the body of Jesus was stolen while the guards slept (cf. Matt. 28:11-15) or that the actual burial site was confused with another, and that the disciples either perpetrated the fraud of Jesus' rising upon a naive public or actually believed they had seen their Lord, i.e., hallucinated.

Together with the increasing emphasis upon the empty tomb as evidence of the resurrection, accent on the corporeality of the risen Jesus in the later Gospels goes hand in hand. This feature is particularly marked in Luke's Gospel, according to which Jesus appears to his disciples and says:

> "Why are you troubled, and why do questionings rise in your hearts? See my hands and my feet, that

> it is I myself; handle me, and see; for a spirit has not flesh and bones as you see that I have" (Luke 24:38-40).

In the same narrative, Jesus, as if finally to allay all doubt (for the disciples "still disbelieved for joy," Luke 24:41), asks:

> "Have you anything here to eat?" They gave him a piece of broiled fish, and he took it and ate before them (Luke 24:41b-43).

The ascension story in Acts 1, though its primary purpose is to indicate that the palpable fellowship with Jesus which his disciples enjoyed immediately after the resurrection must now give way to a new era of the Spirit, still gives large place to that corporeal aspect—"To whom he presented himself alive after his passion by many proofs, appearing to them during forty days, and speaking of the kingdom of God" (Acts 1:3). The same apologetic motifs are present in the Fourth Gospel narratives, though in considerably heightened form, no doubt for the purpose of meeting further refined arguments from the side of pagan and Jewish opponents (cf. John 20:11-18; 19-20; 24-29; 21:4-14).

Aside from the relative absence of such apologetic considerations from Mark's sermon,"[21] no doubt reflecting an earlier, more primitive stage in the church's encounter with her enemies, Mark's purpose is to *announce* the Lord's resurrection. In contrast to those who feel compelled to apologize for or defend the faith at every turn, Mark merely takes a firmer hold on his pulpit, shouts out the news "He is risen!" and leaves the question of the "how" and "by what means" to the theologians of later generations. And by doing so, he makes himself kin to the earliest preachers of the resurrection, whose outline can still be detected in that "gospel" which Paul received, remarkable for its terseness, almost taciturnity, and absence of apologetic:

> For I delivered to you as of first importance what I also received, that Christ died for our sins in accordance with the scriptures, that he was buried, that he was raised on the third day in accordance with the scriptures, and that he appeared to Cephas, then to the twelve (1 Cor. 15:3-5).

Luther's statement to the effect that the evangelists did not bother their heads with historical sequence, that for them everything hangs on the "fruit and use" of Christ's resurrection, or that the "real hot-cross bun" consists in a knowledge of Christ, has its most appropriate application in the case of our preacher, Mark.[22]

That "name above every name," to which the Christ-hymn in Philippians refers, is without doubt the title "Lord." The verse itself (v. 10) is a quotation from the primitive Christian community's "Bible," i.e., the Septuagint or Greek translation of Isaiah 45:23, in which the homage described is paid to God. In other words, in the "hymn," the attributes of deity are clearly ascribed to Christ. Whether or not the earliest community applied the title "Lord" to Christ in a way analogous to the worship of deity in Hellenistic, pagan cults, the use of this verse from Isaiah indicates that

> The Christian community, in a period prior to Paul and under the influence of the Septuagint, gave to this title which it appropriated from its Hellenistic environment, a content which raised Christ above any analogy to pagan cult heroes.[23]

In the Christ-hymn, then, just as God bears the title "Lord," so it is given to Christ to be called "Lord," that is, to possess lordship over the entire cosmos. "Consciously or unconsciously, the world has to do with Christ, insofar as it has to do with God. From now on he is its Ruler and Judge."[24]

If Mark employs this title in a similar fashion, we must look elsewhere than to his resurrection account, for the term appears only in the longer, spurious ending to the Gospel (vv. 19 and 20). From verse 3 of chapter 1 and on, Mark employs the term fourteen times in his sermon. But in each case we are all but in the dark as to whom the title is applied. For example, does the quotation in 1:3 (from the Septuagint translation of Isaiah 40:3, "Prepare the way of the Lord . . . .") refer to God or to the Messiah? In 2:28 ("so the Son of man is lord even of the sabbath") the question is all the more burning inasmuch as the designation "Lord" appears alongside another title capable of being applied to at least three different persons—man as such, Jesus, or another to whom Jesus points.[25] In 5:19, Jesus encourages the man healed of demon possession to go home and tell "how much the Lord has done for you, and how he has had mercy on you." Is the reference to Jesus or to the One who has sent him and whose instrument he is? The situation is every bit as puzzling in each one of the remaining instances (cf. 11:3, 9; 12:9, 11, 29, 30, 36, 37; 13:20, 35), with one exception in which the title is obviously to be translated "Sir," or "milord" (7:28).

In light of the extreme brevity of Mark's resurrection narrative, we should not be chagrined at having to look elsewhere in his sermon to note his variation on the theme of lordship as struck in Philippians 2. If the death-motif gives to the Gospel its "backward" character, it is reasonable to expect that attributes of the risen, exalted Christ should be applied to the story of

Jesus prior to his cross and resurrection. And indeed, it was noted[26] that the resurrection theme was reflected in the storm-narratives of chapters 4 and 6, as well as in the transfiguration account of chapter 9. Mark writes his sermon this side of Easter. But if our assumption that Mark's Gospel is a sermon constructed *a la* such pre-Pauline "hymns" as appear in Philippians, how shall we explain this casual attitude toward a title which for the Greek Old Testament as well as for the Hellenistic Christian community carried the heaviest pay-load of all, a designation which ultimately outdistanced all others originating in Palestine (i.e., "Messiah," "Son of man," "Son of God") and came to sum up the heart and essence of the faith—"Jesus is Lord"?

There are at least three possible explanations. The first is that Mark's use of the title is primitive.[27] That is, despite its appearance in the Greek Old Testament, our preacher employs the term at a period when it has not yet come into its own within the primitive Christian community. Matthew, like Mark, is sparing in his use of the title, though the reason may lie less in Matthew than in his readers for whom other, more specifically Jewish titles carried greater significance. On the other hand, Luke uses the title twelve times of Jesus in narrative material, whereas John applies it, in the main, to the risen Christ. Another explanation is that the ambiguity attaching to the title "Lord" in Mark is due to that same quality of "indirectness" we first noted in connection with his use of the term "Son of God."[28] That it is due, in other words, to Mark's reticence to provide his terms with complete definitions for the sake of moving his hearer-reader to supply those definitions when his total case has been presented. And yet, though the difference between the ambiguity in Mark's use of the title "Son of God" and the lack of clarity in his use of the term "Lord" may prove to be only a difference of degree, the contrast is sharp enough and the instances in which the title "Lord" appear are puzzling enough to suggest another explanation. That explanation, simply put, is that Mark prefers such titles as "Son of God," "Messiah," and "Son of Man," all of which have their roots in Jewish, Palestinian soil, to a term which, originating in the Old Testament name for God, was nonetheless most suitable for challenging as well as for providing a link with pagan, Hellenistic cults.

If, as earlier indicated, the Gospel of Mark is the result of a fusion of the Palestinian "Gospel of Jesus" with the Hellenistic "Gospel about Jesus," to use a famous 19th century distinction, it is reasonable to assume that now one and now another of those two elements will receive the emphasis. It would thus appear that Mark's casual use of the title "Lord" is just the other side of the coin of his preference for Christological titles whose background lay almost entirely within the confines of Jewish messianism. This graphic, giving flesh to such a hymn as Paul incorporates in Philippians 2 by way of Palestinian, Jewish material both constitutes Mark's Gospel a Gospel, the first of its kind, and distinguishes it from that merely formal treatment of the concept "gospel" in Paul.

Thus, for Mark, that name which is above every name is not the title "Lord," but rather "Son of God." Whether or not we are to supply this name with the content with which later centuries of faith and confession have furnished it—equality with God in essence, partaking of the very "stuff" of deity—or must rather view it as somehow synonymous with the title "Christ" or "Messiah"—Jesus lays claim to both in one and the same breath before the Sanhedrin in 14:61 f. The fact remains that for Mark "Son of God" is the loftiest title which may be applied to Jesus. It appears on the lips of those who alone recognize him for what he truly is. Prior to the Passion, and in midst of the confusion reigning about Jesus' identity, a confusion worse confounded by the misunderstanding of his own disciples, the demons, those minions of Satan, the "stronger one" whom he came to bind and whose house he came to plunder, penetrate his incognito and as if to wield a superior power over him by naming his name, acknowledge:

> "You are the Son of God" (3:11)
>
> "What have you to do with me, Jesus, Son of the Most High God?" (5:7).

And at the conclusion of his sermon, after telling that the inscription of the charge against Jesus read, "The King of the Jews" (15:26), and that his scoffers yelled, "Let the Christ, the King of Israel, come down now from the cross" (15:32), Mark, with an infinite artistry which renders each successive title loftier and grander than the one preceding, climaxes his Passion story with the confession of the centurion who saw him breathe his last:

> "Truly this man was a son of God!" (15:39).

Turning now to the last strophe in the Pauline hymn, the obeisance and confession to which Philippians 2: 10-11 refer are not performed by human beings—"it would indeed be more than strange if men were ranged in a series with spiritual powers in heaven and in the underworld"[29]—but rather by forces once hostile to God. Perhaps a quotation from a third century pagan "recipe," designed to give the user power over the spirits holding men under their spell, will help to make this clear:

> "I adjure thee, every daemonic spirit, say whatsoever thou art. For I adjure thee by the seal which Solomon laid upon the tongue of Jeremiah and he spake. And say thou whatsoever thou art, *in heaven, or of the air, or on earth, or under the earth or below the ground . . .*"[30]

The point in these final verses of the "hymn" is that the powers of the air, the earth, and the underworld have found a new Master. Once they were subject to blind fate, to irrevocable destiny, and a man could escape their evil influence only through magical incantation or through astrology by which he sought to read the "stars" which ruled them and thus anticipate their actions. But now the rule of fate has been broken. Jesus has come to occupy the throne which fate once held, and to him all the powers in heaven, earth, and under the earth bow the knee. By ascending his throne, by banishing the "stars" against which not only men but even the "powers" struggled and competed, Jesus has united what once was divided, and has put down the rebellion in the universe and brought peace to the world. Can there be any doubt that the same theme is struck in Mark's portrayal of God's Son, the exorcisor of demons and "Stronger than the strong"? This end of the demons' rule and with it the rule of fate is not some future event to which Mark points forward. Indeed, the apocalyptic passages in his sermon make clear that what is taking place is not the whole of it, that everything runs its inevitable course toward the appearance of the "Son of man" on the clouds of heaven. But this feature does not obscure the fact that Mark intends that Jesus should emerge at once as the One enthroned, as wielder of might over the whole cosmos, as healer and restorer of its divisions and contradictions. This is the meaning of the "kingdom," that puzzling idea which Mark and the Jesus of Mark never bother to define. Where once men and gods tore at each other's flesh for mastery and thus made evil and error and death prevail, now by the one Lord, the Son of God, the kingdom of unity and peace appears, and with it the gifts of healing, forgiveness, and life. If we are justified in construing Mark's sermon after the fashion of that pre-Pauline, Hellenistic hymn, it is small wonder that those "spirits" should see best what can only be intuited by the crowds, should acknowledge to be true what Jesus' enemies can only call a blasphemy, and should understand what his disciples never understood. Their master had been exchanged for Another, and with that exchange their rule was broken.

3.

The Preacher's Secret

Toward Caesarea

We have had occasion to refer to Mark's "indirectness" as preacher, to his penchant for leaving undefined the high titles used of Jesus throughout his sermon. Indeed, at almost every point, but particularly in connection with our evangelist's variants on the themes in lines two to four of the Christ-hymn, we have encountered features which seemed to run completely counter to Mark's portrait of Jesus elsewhere. To tell the truth, so far our exposition of the Gospel has consisted largely of "reading between the lines." It is time now to turn the other side of the coin and to examine this aspect of Mark's sermon which shrouds both the words and the deeds of Jesus in an ambiguity which required such reading, and to arrive at some kind of conclusion regarding Mark's purpose for composing such an ambiguous Gospel.

Through the years it has been customary to refer to this aspect of Mark's Gospel as the "Messianic Secret." And it will soon become clear that the "secret" in Mark is by no means confined to the question of Jesus' messiahship. Rather, it is reflected in every narrative and saying of his sermon. Perhaps there is no better way by which to accent this fact than to leap through the entire Gospel, much as we did in connection with the death-motif—though now working forward rather than backward—and to single out some of the instances in which the idea of the secret appears.

In chapter 1:10, Mark describes Jesus as emerging from his baptism to behold "the heavens opened and the Spirit descending" and hearing a voice from heaven. In apparent contrast to Luke, who seems to make the assembled multitude witness to the vision and voice (cf. Luke 3:21-22), and in certain contrast to the Fourth Evangelist who makes the Baptist witness to the event,[1] the Jesus of Mark is the sole and exclusive audience. Jesus alone sees the Spirit and he alone hears the voice. One need only note that the subject of the sentence in v. 9 is identical with that of v. 10 to recognize the truth of this assertion. Baptized in public, his installation as Servant and Son and his equipment with the Spirit are a secret known only to him. In the same chapter, the larger part of which is more or less designed to describe a typical day's activity, Jesus in the Capernaum synagogue encounters a man with an "unclean spirit" which acknowledges him as the "Holy One of God" only to be rebuked, "Be silent, and come out of him!" (1:24-25).[2]

In a later scene Mark adds the note that Jesus performed many exorcisms but "would not permit the demons to speak, because they knew him" (1:34).[3] The injunctions to silence, then, are for the purpose of concealing Jesus' identity. At the conclusion of the first chapter, the secrecy motif appears in Jesus' peremptory command to the healed leper to "say nothing to any one" (1:44). In chapter 2, following the healing of the paralytic, Mark introduces us for the first time to a title which Jesus continually uses of himself throughout the Gospel, the title "Son of man":

> ". . . But that you may know that the Son of man has authority on earth to forgive sins"—he said to the paralytic—"I say to you, rise, take up your pallet and go home" (2:10-11).[4]

How are we to understand this title? Since Jesus' native tongue was Aramaic, and the Aramaic counterpart of "Son of man," *barnascha,* is customarily translated by the personal pronoun "I," it is justifiable to assume that in certain instances Jesus is simply referring to himself as the subject of an utterance or action. On the other hand, its repeated appearance on the lips of Jesus suggests that by it our preacher intends something more than a mere personal reference. That is, that he wishes to conjure up in the mind of his hearer-reader the figure of the World-judge and Ruler which occupied such large place in Jewish thought between the Testaments. That, further, Mark's purpose in arousing his readers to such a reminiscence is to establish a connection between the apocalyptic Son of man and Jesus himself. An audience acquainted with the popular theology of the day, encountering passages such as Mark 2:10, was bound to recall the word from Daniel 7:

> I saw in the night visions, and behold, with the clouds of heaven there came one like a son of man, and he came to the Ancient of Days and was presented before him. And to him was given dominion and glory and kingdom, that all peoples, nations, and languages should serve him; his dominion is an everlasting dominion, which shall not pass away, and his kingdom one that shall not be destroyed (Dan. 7:13-14).

But what kind of connection are we to establish between Jesus and this Danielic figure? In Mark's "Little Apocalypse," chapter 13, Jesus says:

> "But in those days, after that tribulation, the sun will be darkened, and the moon will not give its light, and the stars will be falling from heaven, and the powers in the heavens will be shaken. And then they will see the Son of man coming in clouds with great power and glory . . . " (13:24-26).

Is Jesus here identifying himself with the Son of man? Or again, in 14:61-62, in reply to the high priest's query, "Are you the Christ, the Son of the Blessed?" Jesus declares:

> "I am; and you will see the Son of man sitting at the right hand of Power, and coming with the clouds of heaven."

How are we to interpret these words? Does Jesus here acknowledge himself to be the Messiah and Son of man in one and the same breath, or does he merely confess to being the Christ and point to the Son of man as to another? This ambiguity which attaches to Jesus' references to the Son of man throughout Mark's sermon makes it well-nigh impossible to settle down with any one definition or interpretation. It is my contention that this ambiguity, which in part may be explained from the fact that a veil of obscurity always lay over the title even before Jesus' use of it, is pressed by Mark into the service of the "Messianic Secret." In other words, in Mark's sermon Jesus' reference to the Son of man is all of a piece with his incognito. That the Christian community these thousand years has identified Jesus with the coming World-ruler and Judge does not erase the fact that within the context of Mark's Gospel no other title is as appropriate to concealing Jesus' identity as that epithet "Son of man."

Again, in chapter 3:11-12, Jesus strictly orders the demons not to make him known. In the same chapter, close on the heels of Mark's description of the reaction of the crowds and of the authorities—"What is this? A new teaching with authority!" (1:27); "Why does this man speak thus? It is blasphemy!" (2:7)[5]—Jesus' own kith and kin are characterized as blind and uncomprehending. In contrast to the RSV translation which speaks of Jesus' "friends" as going out to seize him, "for they said, 'He is beside himself' " (3:21), Old Testament parallels as well as parallels from the apocrypha indicate that the reference is not merely to friends, but to Jesus' own family. The explicit reference to Jesus' "mother and his brothers" at the conclusion of the chapter, as well as Jesus' reply to their inquiries after him, appears to support our contention. In chapter 4, Mark, characteristically, concentrates the majority of parables contained in his sermon. Here it is made crystal-clear that the purpose of Jesus' parables is not to reveal, but to conceal.

The meaning of the parables is explained to the disciples (cf. 4:10 ff., and 34b: "privately to his own disciples he explained everything"), but to the masses he talks in riddles:

> And he said to them, "To you has been given the secret of the kingdom of God, but for those outside everything is in parables . . . " (4:11).

To be sure, the harsh tension between crowds and disciples will some day be relieved:

> "Is a lamp brought in to be put under a bushel, or under a bed, and not on a stand? For there is nothing hid, except to be made manifest; nor is anything secret, except to come to light . . . " (4:21-22; cf. Matt. 10:26-27; Luke 12:2-3).

But that day will only be the day after his resurrection when Jesus' messiahship will be openly proclaimed.

If the purpose of Jesus' parables in Mark is to conceal, that concealment in turn has as its goal the hardening of men's hearts:

> ". . . so that they may indeed see but not perceive, and may indeed hear but not understand; lest they should turn again, and be forgiven" (4:12).

These latter verses are a quotation of Isaiah 6:9 ff., in which God commissions the prophet to make men's hearts fat, their ears heavy, and their eyes shut "until cities lie waste . . . and houses without men, and the land is utterly desolate." In other words, we are to understand the hardening resulting from Jesus' enigmatic speech as willed and intended by God himself. What possible purpose can there be in such a characterization as Mark gives here if it is not to serve the motif of the "secret," and further, to declare it as part and parcel of the divine arrangement of things?

Immediately following his parable section, in his first storm-narrative, Mark brings to shattering climax the questioning of the crowds, the unbelief of Jesus' enemies and the blindness of his own house with a portrait of the disciples as utterly ignorant of his person and power. Earlier, Mark had hinted at their lack of comprehension when he described their inquiry into the meaning of the parables and Jesus' reply, "Do you not understand . . . ?" (4:10 ff.). But after having been given the "secret of the kingdom" and still to persist in their misunderstanding can only mean that the disciples, like all the others, do not know who Jesus is. These two features—Jesus' injunctions to silence and the misunderstanding of the disciples as a kind of climax to the world's unbelief—continue to reappear throughout Mark's sermon, like strophe and antistrophe in an ancient chorus.

In chapter 5:37, Jesus allows only Peter, James, and John to witness the raising of the synagogue ruler's daughter. As already indicated in our discussion of the transfiguration and Gethsemane stories, only these three are privy to his most secret manifestation and inmost self. Of a piece with such "physical" retreats from his audiences are those references to Jesus' removal to lonely places (e.g., 1:35) and his attempts at hiding (e.g., 7:24).[6] The motif of the secret crops up again in the narrative of Jesus' appearance in his native synagogue. His audience, to whom he is only too well known, takes offense at his teaching:

> "Where did this man get all this? What is the wisdom given to him? What mighty works are wrought by his hands! Is not this the carpenter, the son of Mary and brother of James and Joses and Judas and Simon, and are not his sisters here with us?" (6:2b-3).

In the verses following, Herod is described as confusing Jesus with the Baptist (6:14 ff.), and again the disciples in the second storm-scene are exposed as uncomprehending—"for they did not understand about the loaves, but their hearts were hardened" (6:52).

In chapter 7, the disciples inquire into the meaning of Jesus' speech and are upbraided for their lack of understanding (7:17-18). In v. 24, Jesus attempts to remain incognito; in v. 33 he takes the deaf-mute privately aside and after healing him enjoins to silence (v. 36).

Toward Jerusalem

Chapter 8 forms the great caesura or break in Mark's Gospel. Up to it, Jesus carries on an esoteric or private ministry. Away from it, his activity takes on public character. And the "hinge" or binding which holds these contrasting elements of Jesus' ministry together is the confession of Peter at Caesarea Philippi:

> And Jesus went on with his disciples, to the villages of Caesarea Philippi; and on the way he asked his disciples, "Who do men say that I am?" And they told him, "John the Baptist; and others say, Elijah; and others one of the prophets." And he asked them, "But who do you say that I am?" Peter answered him, "You are the Christ" (8:27-29).

Preceding Peter's confession, Jesus refuses the Pharisees a sign from heaven (v. 12), attacks his disciples for their obtuseness (vv. 14-21),[7] and orders the blind man healed to avoid his native village (v. 26: "And he sent him away to his home [i.e., "house," cf. n. 6 on p. 120] saying, 'Do not even enter the village' "). Following that confession, Jesus teaches the multitudes (cf. 8:34 ff.), exorcises a demon in full view of the crowds (9:14 ff.), rides into Jerusalem, cleanses its temple (chapter 11), utters parables whose point is perceived by his enemies (cf. 12:1-12), and goes his way to death observed by all. We might expect, therefore, that Mark's mystery-motif would break off at chapter 8. This is not the case. To be sure, the idea of the secret does not have the stress it receives prior to Caesarea Philippi, but it is still evident. Immediately after Peter's grand declaration, Jesus charges his disciples not to make him known (8:30). From 8:30 and on, Jesus discloses the truth esoterically within the circle of his followers, and in that sense shares the view of the Fourth Evangelist who contrasts the disciples and the ignorant crowds throughout his entire Gospel.

Yet, the disciples still lack comprehension! To

Peter's attempt to dissuade him from his Jerusalem journey Jesus replies, "Get behind me, Satan!" (v. 33). And in the final verse of this chapter, Jesus makes reference to that enigmatic, puzzling Son of man (v. 38). As noted above, Jesus' transfiguration is a private manifestation (9:2 ff.), which he intends to keep secret "until the Son of man should have risen from the dead" (9:9).[8] By virtue of their inability to cure the epileptic boy, the disciples are characterized as faithless (9:17 ff.). In v. 30 of chapter 9, Jesus travels incommunicado and in v. 32 his disciples are portrayed as misunderstanding his second Passion prediction (9:32). In chapter 10, blind Bartimaeus calls "Jesus, Son of David, have mercy on me!" and is rebuked by the disciples and the crowds who tell him to be silent. Admittedly, an attenuated version of the secrecy-motif, but it is present nonetheless. The question concerning Jesus' authority is left unanswered in chapter 11 (vv. 27 ff.) and in 12 he raises a question concerning Messiah's Davidic origin, a virtual dogma of his time:

> "How can the scribes say that the Christ is the son of David? David himself, inspired by the Holy Spirit, declared, 'The Lord said to my Lord, Sit at my right hand, till I put thy enemies under thy feet.' David himself calls him Lord; so how is he his son?" (12:35-37).

Does Jesus here deny Davidic ancestry to Messiah or to himself? Or does he intend rather to attack the quasi-political character of the Messiah with which popular opinion and theology had fitted him out? But if that is so, why did he ride into Jerusalem acknowledging the applause of the crowds:

> "Hosanna! Blessed be he who comes in the name of the Lord! Blessed be the kingdom of our father

> David that is coming! Hosanna in the highest!" (11:9b-10).[9]

The secret still persists! In chapter 13, Jesus announces that following Jerusalem's destruction and the tribulation of the saints there will appear that moment when men "will see the Son of man coming in the clouds with great power and glory" (13:26). Again, does he refer to himself or to another? In 14:3-9, Jesus' messiahship is expressed in the scene at the house of Simon the leper, but in secret, in the *symbolic* action of the woman with the alabaster jar of nard. In the same chapter and the chapter following, Jesus is silent before his accusers (14:61), and the other side of that coin is represented by the disciples' abandonment and flight (14:50) and lastly, by Peter's denial (14:66-72). Silent before Pilate (15:4-5), his release enjoyed by another whose name, ironically (accidentally?) may be translated "Son of the Father," i.e., Bar-abbas (vv. 6-11), he cries, "My God, my God, why hast thou forsaken me?" only to have his prayer misunderstood—"Behold, he is calling Elijah" (vv. 34-35).

He dies. And with that dying the greatest question mark of all is drawn over the portrait of Jesus. Is this crucified, slain Jesus the Messiah who would mount the pinnacle of Jerusalem's temple and announce the time of deliverance to Israel, liberate her from foreign rule, wreak vengeance upon her enemies, compel her allies to pay her tribute, and establish a golden age of peace, reigning in a city which descends in infinite glory from heaven to earth? Is he the one to return the scattered remnants from Mesopotamia and Egypt to their homeland, purge the *yetzer harah,* the "evil impulse," from Israel's heart, make all men prophets, and transform the theaters and circuses of Rome into theological seminaries? As far as I know, only once does the idea of Messiah's death appear in Jewish print, in an apocryphal piece from the close of the first century A.D.:

> "For my son the Messiah shall be revealed with those who are with him, and those who remain shall rejoice four hundred years. And after these years my son the Messiah shall die, and all who draw human breath" (2 Esdras 7:28-29).

But as the verses indicate, that death shall follow the four hundred years of his reign. Where and how did this humiliated Jesus reign? In the rest of Jewish literature suffering and death are predicated either of some lesser, temporary or provisional "Messiah" and not of God's Holy One, or such Old Testament passages which the Christian community has interpreted of Messiah's death (e.g., Psalm 22) are transformed into their opposite. Jewish resistance to the idea of Messiah's death is summed up in the reply of Trypho the Jew to the attempts of the second-century church father Justin Martyr to prove its necessity:

> It has indeed been proved sufficiently by your Scriptural quotations that it was predicted in the Scriptures that Christ should suffer, and that He should come again in glory to accept the eternal kingdom over all nations, and that every kingdom should be made subject to Him. But what we want you to prove is that this Jesus is the Christ spoken of in the Scriptures.[10]

> We are indeed aware that He was to endure suffering, and to be led as a sheep to the slaughter. But what we want you to prove to us is that He was to be crucified and to be subjected to so disgraceful and shameful a death (which even in the Law is

> cursed). We find it impossible to think that this could be so.[11]

Small wonder that this resistance should be reflected scores of times in apostolic preaching and teaching:

> Christ died for our sins in accordance with the scriptures (1 Cor. 15:3).
>
> "Have you come out as against a robber . . . ? Day after day I sat in the temple teaching, and you did not seize me. But all this has taken place, that the scriptures of the prophets might be fulfilled" (Matt. 26:55-56).
>
> ". . . Was it not necessary that the Christ should suffer these things and enter into his glory?" (Luke 24:26).
>
> But one of the soldiers pierced his side with a spear, and at once there came out blood and water. . . . For these things took place that the scripture might be fulfilled, "Not a bone of him shall be broken." And again another scripture says, "They shall look on him whom they have pierced" (John 19:34-37).

And in light of this reaction, it is no surprise that Mark's narrative of the Passion should read more like an anthology of Old Testament passages than a news item. All of this only serves to underscore the truth that apart from his ambiguous self-designation, his incognito, his injunctions to silence, and the lack of apprehension on the part of crowds, ecclesiastical authorities, family, and disciples, the death of Jesus is the darkest veil of all thrown over his identity. The secret is not even broken by the narrative of his resurrection, for those to whom it is announced are too frightened to relate it (16:8).

The Mystery and the Call to Faith

What possible purpose can Mark have had in employing such a motif? The tradition upon which he drew in order to give graphic substance to the Hellenistic theme of descent-humiliation and ascent-exaltation either did not contain it or contained it only to a degree. This is evident from the fact that on occasion Mark notes exceptions to the rule. For example, in 1:45, the leper disobeys Jesus' prohibition and broadcasts his healing to such degree that "Jesus could no longer openly enter a town . . . " (1:43 ff.). In 4:21, to which Matthew 10:26-27 and Luke 12:2-3 furnish parallels,[12] Jesus declares that nothing is hid but to be made manifest, nothing secret but to come to light. In 5:19, Jesus is described as violating his own principle in his command to the demoniac to "go home to your friends, and tell them how much the Lord has done for you . . . ." Chapter 7 records Jesus' inability to remain incommunicado (7:24), and at the chapter's end witnesses to the healing of the deaf-mute more zealously spread the news the more sternly Jesus charges them to keep it secret. The same is true of Bartimaeus in chapter 10:48. Upon being rebuked, he cries all the more, "Son of David, have mercy on me!" If these exceptions to Mark's motif were already present in the tradition, it is possible that he had no choice but to allow them, since any other course would have brought his sermon under suspicion. It is also possible that these exceptions to the motif of the secret are simply the expression of our preacher's inability to fasten upon one theme and carry it forward consistently, or of his unsuccessful attempts at a higher and grander concept of the Christ, similar, perhaps, to the portrait of Jesus in the Fourth Gospel. This latter view has found acceptance with at least one Gospel commentator:

> St. Mark is inclined to overstep the limits prescribed by his doctrine of the secret and to delineate the incarnate life openly in terms of the apostolic faith. Hence certain passages convey the impression that the true nature of Jesus is reaching out for some definite form of articulate expression which, however, it cannot yet receive.[13]

Yet, as one scholar put it some sixty years ago, if Mark had consistently executed his view of the mystery, the Gospel would scarcely have been worth telling! The Jesus who worked publicly and made himself known was the object of his Gospel. The Jesus who hid himself could not really be described.[14] In other words, Mark includes these exceptions by design, with or without thought for the tradition which might have contained them. They are an integral part of his sermon. Without them, the portraits of the hidden, humiliated Jesus and the colossal Son of God would have stood in an intolerable contradiction. For the sake of his hearer-reader, the motif of the mystery requires interruption, it requires violation so as to do service to the theme of the "Mightier One."

> That Jesus' real intention was frustrated cannot be what Mark intends to say . . . [Jesus'] glory breaks forth by the fact that he wishes to remain hidden and yet is confessed. . . . Every such confession is a witness to Jesus. He thereby gains recognition in the eyes of the narrator as well as in the eyes of the reader.[15]

Returning to our original question, the purpose of Mark's secrecy-motif, I am of the conviction that without it his Gospel would be merely a *"bios,"* a life of Jesus. To be sure, a life or story of incomparable grandeur; at bottom, however, a reminiscence or memoir and little more. But Mark intends his Gospel to be a "gospel," that is, a proclamation which encounters the hearer and calls him to respond in faith to the One it announces. And since faith is the answer of the total person, the gospel can be nothing less than an appeal to the "free verdict of the human heart." It cannot be a mere narration of significant events in the life of Jesus to which the mind may give assent. Nor can it compel or overwhelm.

The gospel must appear as "parable," at one and the same time revealing and concealing.[16] It must announce the truth without insisting that that truth can be known or recognized through sheer sense perception or any of the common, human ways of knowing. For Mark, this means portraying the Christ of God veiled in the misunderstood, humiliated Jesus of Nazareth. It means preaching by indirection, employment of the motif of the mystery. This motif is not our preacher's subtle invention, superimposed upon the biblical record for the purpose of convincing a skeptical audience that the reason no one recognized Jesus as God's Messiah was that he traveled in disguise.[17] Mark had his theme of the mystery literally served up to him—in the cross. Whatever temporary losses Jesus may have sustained during his lifetime could be recouped. But his cross and death drew a great question mark over his entire career. Old Testament passages adduced to prove that all that happened happened according to the "definite plan and foreknowledge of God" sufficed to convince only those who already believed that behind the scorn of Jesus' enemies, behind the rattling spear, the hammer's stroke, behind all that blood and death God himself stood within the shadows, hidden, but "keeping watch above his own." It is the cross and not our preacher which throws the veil over his Colossus and which makes of his sermon a "parable," a riddle. What was left to Mark was merely to draw a larger shadow for that cross so as to encompass the whole of Jesus' life. And by describing such a shadow, Mark finds himself in the company of the Apostle to the Gentiles who saw in the "word of the cross" the only means for eliciting man's free response:

> Where is the wise man? Where is the scribe? Where is the debater of this age? Has not God made foolish the wisdom of the world? For since, in the wisdom of God, the world did not know God through wisdom, it pleased God through the folly of what we preach to save those who believe. For Jews demand signs and Greeks seek wisdom, but we preach Christ crucified, a stumbling-block to Jews and folly to Gentiles, but to those who are called, both Jews and Greeks, Christ the power of God and the wisdom of God (1 Cor. 1:20-25).

Like Paul before him, Mark is a theologian of the cross. To be sure, the mystery requires penetrating now and again for the sake of the "parable," the sermon, the proclamation which must both reveal and conceal, and hence for the sake of the hearer-reader who must supply the answer to that question, "Who do you say that I am?" freely and without compulsion. But in the last analysis, the mystery is nothing but a symbol of the activity of God himself who dons the servant-form and offers himself alike to faith and unbelief.

To my mind, one of the most beautiful descriptions of that activity of God and hence of that mystery to be found outside Scripture itself is contained in a "poem" by Søren Kierkegaard. A king once loved a humble maiden, but was vexed with doubt. Would she be happy in the life at his side? Would she be able to summon confidence enough never to remember what the king wished only to forget, that he was king and she only a humble maiden? If this memory were to waken in her, where would be the glory of their love? In that case, she would have been happier had she remained in her obscurity. But this would not satisfy the king—he loved her! He could show himself to the maid in all the pomp of his power and make her forget herself in a worshipful admiration. And indeed, this might satisfy the maiden, but it could not satisfy the king who desired her glorification, not his. The only course for him was to become the equal of such a one, to don the habit of the humblest man and thus to run the risk of rejection. Next, contrasting the king, whose beggar-cloak flutters loosely about him only to betray him, with God's true servant-form, Kierkegaard writes:

> Behold where he stands—God! Where? There; do you not see him? He is God; and yet he has not a resting place for his head. . . . He is God; and yet he picks his steps more carefully than if angels guided them. . . . He is God; and yet his eye surveys mankind with anxious care. . . . How wonderful a life, all sorrow and all love; to yearn to express the equality of love and yet to be misunderstood. . . . To sustain the heavens and the earth by the fiat of his omnipotent word, so that if this word were withdrawn for the fraction of a second the universe would be plunged into chaos—how light a task compared with bearing the burden that mankind may take offense, when one has been constrained by love to become its saviour![18]

Mark, more clearly than all the rest, sees the risk, the scandal of the cross and proclaims it more boldly than all. For Luke the cross is only a temporary reversal. Set within the larger scheme of God's activity hastening onward to its goal—the outpouring of the Spirit, the mission of the church—its significance consists merely in the momentary deflection from that goal. Not once is the death of Jesus connected with the forgiveness of sins in Luke's Gospel. Indeed, Mark 10:45—"For the Son of man also came not to be served but to serve, and to give his life as a ransom for many"—is eliminated. In Matthew's Gospel, the sole reference to the Suffering Servant's "bearing our griefs" (Matt. 8:17; cf. Isa. 53:4) is applied not to the idea of forgiveness, but to the healing of physical infirmities. In the Fourth Gospel, the cross is set within the context of Jesus' glorification. On the night of his betrayal and arrest he prays, "Father, the hour has come; glorify thy Son that the Son may glorify thee" (John 17:1b). The cross casts no long, dark shadow over Jesus' ministry. From the very beginning he emerges full-blown as Revealer. Men disbelieve and the disciples misunderstand, not, however, because his deity is hidden or his fateful journey to Jerusalem throws his mission in doubt, but rather because they are blind. And if we were to distinguish Mark's view of Jesus' death from the view contained in the Philippians' "hymn," it would be at the point of Mark's unrelieved concentration upon the death in contrast to the hymn's all but unrestrained joy. To be sure, the hymn comes down hard on Jesus' death as an act of voluntary service, and it is but a step from such an idea to Mark's (and Paul's) concept of the cross as scandal,[19] but the difference is at least one step wide.

4.

The Pew

Every preacher has his audience. Mark was not without his. According to majority opinion, our preacher wrote for non-Jewish readers outside Palestine. For this reason, he translated Aramaic or Hebrew expressions such as *talitha cumi* in 5:41 and explained Jewish customs as in 7:3 f. Older churchly tradition speaks of the Gospel's composition in Rome or somewhere in Italy. A certain "Latin" flavor in Mark's language would appear to agree with this tradition. Such words as "census" in 12:14 and "centurion" in 15:39 are (as, indeed are our English terms) a mere transliteration of the Latin into Greek. These "Latinisms," however, are not to be overevaluated, for Mark's sermon betrays a marked Jewish or Semitic coloring as well.[1]

More important for us is the peculiar shape or form which Mark's hearer-reader gave to his faith and which might single him out from the addressees of Matthew's or Luke's Gospel. In all probability Mark's audience was composed of Roman or at least Italian Christians. But we are concerned with the question, What kind of Christians are such as Mark addresses, be they Roman or Florentine? What are their experiences; what disappointments and frustrations do they encounter; who are their enemies; how do they worship, etc.?

Certainly authors' works reveal something of themselves. We have spent the great part of this little volume concentrating upon the peculiar theology and point of view of Mark. At the same time, it is not impossible that through his piece an author should reveal something of the persons or community to which he is writing. A word here and there, a certain stress or tone, the peculiar nuance given a narrative or speech often betrays the climate of thought, the practices, the needs, and the objections of a man's audience. To cite one instance, those questions which Paul literally shovels out to his reader in his Letter to the Romans cannot be purely rhetorical—"Then what advantage has the Jew? Or what is the value of circumcision?" (Rom. 3:1); "What then shall we say about Abraham, our forefather according to the flesh?" (4:1); "What shall we say then? Are we to continue in sin that grace may abound?" (6:1); "What then shall we say? That the law is sin?" (7:7); "I ask then, has God rejected his people?" (11:1), etc., etc. Though Paul's arguments in these passages are written in a style familiar to his time (i.e., after the manner of the Cynic-Stoic diatribe), they nevertheless answer to questions and perplexities raised and suffered by friends and enemies. Mark's style is certainly not Paul's, and for that reason the character of his audience does not appear to be so clearly reflected. It is possible, nonetheless, to glean from Mark's sermon something of a portrait of his hearer-reader.

There are at least five areas in which the character and experience of Mark's community appear to be reflected. Proceeding from the general to the more specific and peculiar, they may be classified as the Life of the Believer; the Enemy; the Problem of Fellowship; Techniques for Evangelists, and Reflections of Ritual.

The Life of the Believer

Leafing through the Gospel, it is possible, I believe, to uncover hints and clues to the situation-in-life of Mark's hearer-reader in regard to his experience of faith. Naturally, much of what is reflected here will be the common experience of all Christians. My goal is simply to point up such reflection.

If it is unwarranted to assume that the first thirteen verses of Mark's Gospel which relate John's preaching, Jesus' baptism and temptation are modeled after the believer's existence, it is appropriate to see in those events the type of the believer's life of faith. With little exception the career of Mark's hearer, at least in its initial stages, followed the pattern of the narrative set down in 1:1-13. First the Good News was announced. We need merely compare a few of the sermon-stereotypes in the Book of the Acts to realize that the call to repentance and proffer of forgiveness preceded every other missionizing activity (cf. the Pentecost sermon of Acts 2; Peter's words at the portico of Solomon in 3:19; the word of Simon in 8:22, and Paul's Areopagus speech in 17:30-31). Then followed confession, baptism, and the reception of the Spirit, for the most part in that order (cf. the exception in Acts 10:44 ff., in which the reception of the Spirit is described as preceding the baptism).

If immediately upon his "inauguration" Jesus engaged in struggle with the tempter, those newly baptized into the primitive Christian community were ultimately if not immediately vulnerable to the appeal to don their old habit of life or to replace their new confession with another. The Galatian community found itself in precisely this situation, and Paul expressed chagrin at the fact that "[they] were so quickly deserting him who called [them] in the grace of Christ and turning to a different gospel . . . " (Gal. 1:6). Call, baptism, and temptation were not a sequence peculiar to the career of Mark's hearer. Such is the universal stuff of Christian existence. Nor is the sequence peculiar to Mark. Matthew and Luke also begin their narrative of Jesus' ministry with John's preaching, the baptism, and the temptation. In the latter Gospels, however, the stories of Jesus' birth throw an other-worldly shadow over a succession of events which in Mark appear to enjoy such close correspondence with the believer's own experience. At any rate, the similarity in the synoptic accounts as well as the universality of the believer's existence which they reflect ought not to rob us, if not Mark's original audience, of taking comfort in the fact that our own life of faith has its counterpart in the life of Christ.

Earlier[2] we noted that the suddenness of the disciples' response to Jesus' call in 1:18 and 20 carried overtones reminiscent of the creative word in Genesis 1:3. At the same time, if the speed of the disciples' reply does not correspond with the haste with which the Jewish and pagan world appropriated the Good News, it certainly answers to the type of response to which Mark calls his hearer. In a time made urgent by the expectation of the imminent return of Christ to judgment, Mark expects that the same haste by which he characterized the answer of Peter, James, John, Levi, and the Twelve should mark the reply of his hearer to his own proclamation—"And immediately they left their nets and followed him" (1:18); "And immediately he called them; and they left their father Zebedee in the boat . . ." (1:20); "He saw Levi the son of Alphaeus sitting at the tax office, and he said to him, 'Follow me.' And he rose and followed him" (2:14);

"And he went up into the hills, and called to him those whom he desired; and they came to him" (3:13).

More to the point of our discussion is the word concerning the bridegroom and the double-parable of the wine and the patch in 2:18-22, which together provide the answer to the fasting question: "Why do John's disciples and the disciples of the Pharisees fast, but your disciples do not fast?" By the time Mark had penned his sermon, the Christian community was already encountering sects or the beginnings of sects in which figures other than Jesus were venerated if not worshiped. The situation suggested by these verses is a veneration of John the Baptist which reached its climax in the second century. For the Christian community the question would naturally arise as to the relationship between John and Jesus. Were their teachings in any way to be regarded as complementary or as antithetical? In the bridegroom speech, Jesus repudiates the custom of fasting as such. He announces that the time has come; the bridegroom has chosen his bride, the troth has been plighted, and the wedding is not far off. The sons of the bridechamber stand ready to accompany the bride to the home of her husband with song and dancing. It is hence a time for joy, a time in which fasting—symbolic of mourning caused by separation—can have no place. It is certainly a more august claim than the claim to messiahship which Mark makes here on Jesus' behalf. Fasting is inappropriate because Jahve, the bridegroom of Hosea 2:21 and Isaiah 54:5, is in the midst, gathering his elect! In the double-parable, Jesus declares that if an attempt were made to combine his way of life with that of the Baptist, the result would be equal to sewing a new patch on old cloth, or pouring new wine into old skins.

To his hearer, perplexed by the continuance of

schools and sects and systems coexisting with the new community, Mark thus announces that there is a force at work in Jesus which is not present in the old order —characterized by Pharisee and Baptist—and which makes such coexistence impossible. Combination of the traditional and familiar with the new brought by Jesus can only result in destruction—"the wine will burst the skins, and the wine is lost, and so are the skins . . . " (2:22). It is possible that the same idea is present in 1:14, which clearly separates the activity of the Baptist from that of Jesus: "Now after John was arrested, Jesus came into Galilee, preaching . . . ." Not until the period of the Fourth Evangelist, however, is so clear a line of demarcation drawn between Jesus and John. In Mark's sermon, as noted earlier,[3] the figures of Jesus and the Baptist merge so as to include John within the time of salvation. But we can be relatively certain that the Baptist "sect" had already emerged at the time of Mark's writing. In verse 20 of chapter 2, we encounter the reference to the bridegroom's departure, no doubt intended by Mark to be a presage of Jesus' death—"The days will come, when the bridegroom is taken away from them, and then they will fast in that day." Whether or not we are to read into these words justification for Friday fasts is doubtful. But it is interesting to note that the *Syrian Didascalia,* written in approximately A.D. 250, cites this passage in support of Christians' fasting simultaneously with the Jews at Passover, a custom observed by the so-called Quartodecimans:

> . . . in the days of the Pascha, wherein all the faithful throughout the world fast; as our Lord and Teacher said when they asked him: "Why do John's disciples fast, but thine fast not? . . . "[4]

In 3:31-35 as well as in 10:28-31, scenes are related which appear to touch an area of Mark's hearer-reader's concern. In the first narrative, Mark records that Jesus' mother and brothers were inquiring after him, upon which Jesus turns to those about him and says, "Here are my mother and my brothers! Whoever does the will of God is my brother, and sister, and mother." In the second narrative, to Peter's statement that the disciples have left all to follow, Jesus replies that none who has left house, brothers, sisters, mother, father, children, or lands for his sake or the gospel's will not receive a hundredfold in this time, with persecutions, and in the age to come eternal life. Dare we see in these scenes a reflection of Gentile-Christian embarrassment in face of the religious heritage of Judaism, a possible "inferiority complex" on the part of those converted from paganism in contrast to their Jewish-Christian counterparts who boasted in the law, the prophets, and in their natural descendence from Abraham? Racism is hardly a modern phenomenon. It flourished in antiquity. Suppose, then, that our preacher addressed himself to his hearers' envy in a word which announced that the family of God consisted in an obedience to his will which transcended the ties of blood. If pride of origin furnished a barrier to Israel's reception of the message of John (cf. Matt. 3:9 and Luke 3:8), as well as of Jesus (cf. John 8:33, 39), it is not surprising that the same boast on behalf of *Blut und Boden* should threaten the life of the Christian community. As Romans 11:18 indicates, boasting was not confined to the Jew, but in these two scenes Mark, via a word of Jesus, appears intent on lifting the question of kinship beyond the sphere to which pride and envy are normally native.

Within the Gospel many of the speeches of Jesus,

which Mark no doubt gleaned from his Palestinian sources, deserve—apart from their original, historical setting—to be regarded as reflections of "rules" governing the life of the Christian community. Jesus' words concerning divorce (10:2-9, 10-12); riches (10:23 ff.); the widow's mite (12:41-44); God and Caesar (12:13-17)—to name but a few—all correspond to situations prevailing in Mark's and his hearer's lifetime. In the period of the Empire, divorce was an easy matter—Caesar had four wives, Sulla and Pompey had five. It was an era for which the sexual was as incidental to the totality of a man's life as eating or drinking. In Mark 10:11 Jesus declares that a man who divorces his wife and marries another commits adultery. In the verse following, however, he applies the same dictum to the wife. Such words appear to refract a type of marriage contract popularized in the Roman imperial period, according to which the bride remained under her father's jurisdiction even after her marriage. This granting of "women's rights" over against husbands who could not dispose of their property led only to an intensification of the divorce rate, given the universal moral laxity. As to the economic conditions in Mark's time, the gap between rich and poor was great. Only one estate, the rich, had money enough to erect the buildings whose ruins we visit today. A solid middle class was lacking; the masses lived in squalor. From these masses came the bulk of the earliest Christian community, the poor, the orphan, and the widow whom Jesus praised in 12:41 ff., a rabble society from which the wealthy turned away—"How hard it will be for those who have riches to enter the kingdom of God!" What Paul writes of the composition of the congregation at Corinth, i.e., that not many wise after the flesh, not many influential, not many of high degree are called

(1 Cor. 1:26), summarizes the economic conditions regnant in all the congregations of the Roman empire.

As for God and Caesar, it is difficult to tell to what degree the invocation of the heathen gods or of the deified emperor affected the Christians of New Testament times. We know that public life in the cities was so closely bound up with participation in heathen cults that Christians undoubtedly came into serious difficulties. By refusing to invoke the gods—and only in the context of such a worship did veneration of the emperor have any real significance — the Christian estranged himself from the citizenry. He was regarded as not merely "godless" but as unpatriotic, subversive. The state could not tolerate the holding of opinions deviating from the majority view. To give Caesar what was Caesar's, rightfully Caesar's from the viewpoint of the gospel, could conceivably land one in the arena.

The three Passion predictions in 8:31 ff., 9:31 ff., and 10:32 ff., beyond focusing upon the event in Jesus' life which was most signal for Mark, intend to portray the life of the believer as well. Should there be any doubt in the matter, the fact that Mark has immediately appended to the first Passion prediction Jesus' call to his disciples and to the multitude to take up their cross ought to dispel it. Mark's hearer is here enjoined to undergo martyrdom, whether "white" or "red," not, however, in imitation of the sufferings and death of Jesus. The invitation is not to imitate, but rather to "follow" him (v. 34). Mark thus confronts his hearer-reader with two possibilities, two kinds of life. What shall a man do to live? Kill himself! That is, surrender up his "I," pronounce the death sentence on his desire to be for himself, be his own man, and, if need be, suffer literally the death of a criminal. What shall a man do to die? Live to himself!

> ". . . For whoever would save his life will lose it; and whoever loses his life for my sake and the gospel's will save it . . ." (v. 35).

Unwillingness to die the kind of death, to live the kind of life to which Jesus calls can only mean "taking offence," or as the RSV puts it, being "ashamed" of him (v. 38). And, in one of the most striking utterances in the whole of synoptic tradition, Jesus, whether or not we interpret him as identifying himself with the "Son of man," nevertheless so binds the future of that enigmatic figure to men's present attitude toward himself as to declare:

> ". . . For whoever is ashamed of me and of my words in this adulterous and sinful generation, of him will the Son of man also be ashamed, when he comes in the glory of his Father with the holy angels" (v. 38).

If for Mark the Gospel culminates in the death of Christ, the cross is also the end and goal of the believer's existence. Discipleship can only mean going one's own dusty way to death.[5]

That piece of Mark's Gospel which perhaps more than any other reflects the situation and mentality of his hearer is the so-called "Little Apocalypse" of chapter 13. Whether our preacher appropriated an originally Jewish tract and fused it with the tradition about Jesus; whether he combined with that tradition the predictions of some later, Christian "prophet," or whether, as I am inclined to believe, the entire chapter is built on a foundation attributable to Jesus himself, the chapter clearly reflects the tensions, distresses, and hopes of Mark's community. Indeed, one writer goes so far as to assert that the entire Gospel is written for a community embroiled in the Roman-Jewish war, and which awaits the return of Christ in Galilee.[6] Whatever the original condition of the discourse, Jesus' admonitions to "take heed" (vv. 5, 9, 23, 33) and to "watch" (vv. 33, 35, 37), together with their striking parallel in the Gethsemane scene—"Watch and pray that you may not enter into temptation," 14:38—his promise of the Spirit's help in the "hour" of trial (v. 11); his warning against misinterpreting the signs (vv. 5-8; 21-23) and his promise that the tribulations of the elect will culminate in his appearing and their victory (vv. 13-20, 24-27) all reflect a community harassed by a host of tragic events (Caligula's attempt to erect his image in the Jerusalem temple in A.D. 39-40? The Parthian wars? The famine in Palestine? Earthquakes in Asia?) and longing for the return of its Lord. Its only weapon in the midst of these "woes" is its watchfulness. Indeed, since the Son himself is ignorant of the day or hour of his final appearing (v. 32), his disciples can only be admonished to take heed.

The Enemy

Throughout Mark's sermon we encounter clusters of "conflict-speeches," i.e., debates between Jesus and his opponents on a point of Jewish doctrine or practice. In 2:23—3:6, Jesus contends with the Pharisees concerning the Sabbath; in 3:22-30 with the scribes regarding his exorcism of unclean spirits; in 7:1-23 with scribes and Pharisees in respect of the rites of purification and the Fourth Commandment. The "concealment" view of Jesus' parables in chapter 4 has Jewish opposition to the gospel as its proper background. Jesus' cursing of the fig tree in 11:12-14, 20-26; the cleansing of the temple in 11:15-19; his judgment upon the scribes' scrambling for places of honor in 12:38-40, and his prophecy of the temple ruin in 13:1-8, to say nothing of the descriptions of the ecclesiastical authorities' continual plots against his life, culminating in his cross and death, are only further reflection of Jewish hostility. To what degree this hostility was also experienced by Mark's community can only be surmised. It is not impossible that such scenes as that recorded in 6:1-6, according to which Jesus encounters opposition from his own countrymen (note especially vv. 5-6: "And he could do no mighty work there . . . . And he marveled because of their unbelief"), are a clue to the disappointment and harassment to which primitive Christian missionaries were subject.

Such asides as Mark gives in 7:3-4 concerning Pharisaic meticulousness in the matter of ritual observance may well reflect a certain pique at Jewish intransigence. Years ago, one scholar insisted that such comments were positive proof that Mark's Gospel represented an extreme type of "Paulinism," which held all Jewish distinctions in contempt.[7] As we were careful to note earlier,[8] no literary relationship between Paul and our Gospel can be established, but it is not inconceivable that the Roman Christians eventually came to adopt the apostle as a model, whose appreciation of Jewish scruple may have been overlooked in their zeal to imitate him in all things.

The Problem of Fellowship

A theological problem of profound importance to the earlier community dealt with the question of the mission among the Gentiles, and the attendant problem of Jewish-Gentile fellowship. It is clear from the story of the Syrophoenician woman in 7:24-30 that for our preacher, membership in the Christian family involved submission to the rule of Israel's priority. To the woman's plea to cast the demon out of her daughter Jesus replies, "Let the children first be fed" (v. 27), an obvious reference to the primacy of the Jews within the divine scheme of things. (Do we find here an echo of Romans 1:16?) On the other hand, if any clue is to be gleaned from 2:15-17, in which Jesus is described as sitting at table with sinners and tax collectors, it is obvious that for Mark neither occupation nor prior religious background furnishes a barrier to fellowship within the community.

At the very least, Jesus' reply to his disciples that the stranger exorcising demons in his name ought not to be prohibited (9:38-41) enunciates a principle of toleration toward Christian "outsiders." When we consider that the community to which Paul addressed himself in his Epistle to the Romans consisted of Jewish-Christian circles (out of which the community may once have originated) and whose peculiarities continually threatened that community's life (Rom. 14:1—15:13), as well as of self-conscious Hellenistic groups which presumed on their possession of the Spirit (Rom. 11:18, 12:3, 16; 14:3), we can readily agree that the issue of fellowship between Jew and Gentile was a live one.

Techniques for Evangelists

In the majority of the exorcisms and healings narrated in Mark's Gospel, the component pieces of each scene are relatively constant throughout. Such components have a certain stereotyped quality, and it is the contribution of the historian of forms or species of Gospel material to have indicated the value of such stereotypes for the handing down of the tradition. For example, in every instance Mark notes the type of seriousness of the disease concerned; in each case Jesus applies a word or touch to the person afflicted (the woman with the hemorrhage is not an exception, since her healing is finally confirmed by a word of Jesus, cf. 5:34); where exorcisms are recorded a struggle often ensues (cf. 1:26; 5:7, 10; 9:20) and the dramatic result is noted. Finally, in all but a few instances the crowds, the disciples, or the healed furnish the "chorus" which celebrates the cure (in 3:6 the "chorus" is replaced with the Pharisees' and Herodians' plot against Jesus, and in 5:30 Jesus alone perceives the cure of the woman with the flow of blood). Only a few narratives lack the "chorus" (e.g., the healing of Simon's mother-in-law in 1:30 ff., the blind man in 8:22 ff., and Bartimaeus in 10:46 ff.). Aside from their value as aids to memorization and hence to transmission, such stereotypes could reflect the techniques employed by those members of the Christian community to whom the tasks of healing and exorcism were committed. There is ample evidence that such persons played a considerable role in the primitive church (cf. 1 Cor. 12:9, 28), and it would not be a surprise to encounter a Gospel writer such as Mark providing them a model from out of the Jesus-tradition.

In concluding this little rubric, we ought to note a singular usage of the term "word" in Mark's Gospel, the purpose of which could be to furnish the evangelist of his time with a model or pattern for his preaching. In the Greek text of 1:45 it is said of the leper whom Jesus heals that he "began . . . to spread the word." It may be, as the RSV implies, that it was not the gospel which the leper proclaimed, but simply the "news" of his healing. The quasi-technical character of the term throughout the balance of Mark's sermon, however, suggests that the case for the RSV translation is not "open and shut." For example, in 2:2 Jesus is described as preaching "the word," obviously an abbreviation of what Mark earlier calls "the gospel of God," the content of which is the announcement that God's Rule has broken in (1:14-15). Or again, in the allegorical interpretation of the parable of the sower in chapter 4 (vv. 14-20, an appendage which already existed in Mark's source; cf. also Matt. 13:18-23; Luke 8:11-15), we encounter the term "word" in the absolute sense no less than eight times. In v. 33 of the same chapter, Jesus' preaching is again described as a speaking "the word." In 10:22, the Greek text of Mark describes the rich man as having been saddened by "the word." In the spurious ending of the Gospel, Jesus is said to have corroborated "the word" of his disciples with attendant signs (16:20). Aside from passages in which the term refers merely to the content of conversation (5:36; 7:29; 12:13 and 14:39) or to a question (11:29), in only one instance does the context require that "the word" refer to Mosaic law (7:13). As a rule, "the word" or a close relative ("my words," 8:38; 13:31; "his words," 10:24) appears to be a technical term for "the gospel," the "Good News."

The question as to whether or not, beyond his early definition in 1:14-15, Mark's use of the term lays down a pattern for the preachers of his community can be answered in the affirmative, and on the basis of such passages as 8:32 and 9:10. In neither of these verses does the RSV translate the Greek term. It merely paraphrases. But in both cases we encounter the designation "word" in that absolute sense as noted above. Further, the content which the context in both instances provides that little term is the suffering, death, and rising of Jesus. Here, it appears to me, Mark summarizes the essence of the gospel for the train of preachers and evangelists to follow. The fact that the real axis about which Mark's sermon turns is the cross and death of the Son of God-Messiah-Son of man gives support to our argument. The difference, then, between Mark and Paul, for whom the gospel is eminently summarized in terms of the cross or the "word of the cross" (cf. 1 Cor. 1:18), is that whereas Paul is content to leave that "word" or "gospel" to the area of the conceptual, accenting its implications for the faith and life of the believer, Mark presses the tradition of the words and deeds of Jesus into the service of "the word," and thus gives to the gospel its graphic, pictorial character. From this standpoint, Mark may be viewed as the originator of this genre of primitive Christian literature. Indeed, it can be argued that in light of the great difference between Matthew, Luke, and Mark in this respect, only our preacher's sermon is in a true sense a "Gospel."

Reflections of Ritual

Through the years, considerable attention has been given to possible reflections of primitive Christian ritual in Mark's Gospel. In 1952, Philip Carrington, Archbishop of Quebec, proposed that the Gospel had been composed so as to be read Sunday by Sunday in accordance with the Jewish calendar.[9] Carrington thus arranged the text of the Gospel in light of his "liturgical theory," and later published a "running commentary"[10] in which, among other things, he related the calendrical sequence to the Gospel's thought-background. One of the most recent studies in Mark attempts to demonstrate that what provided the pattern for the whole of his Gospel was the Jewish Passover Haggadah, the story of Israel's deliverance at the hand of Moses. The Gospel is thus to be viewed as a "new Passover Haggadah" in which Jesus is portrayed as fulfilling the promise of Israel's deliverance.[11]

Any attempt to find a consistent pattern in Mark's Gospel, whether it be in the nature of a liturgical theory, a Haggadah theory, or a "sermon" theory, is bound to have about it the air of the synthetic or artificial. In this connection, however, we ought to take note of a few of the aspects of Mark's sermon which appear to reflect the ancient rites of the primitive community and from which such scholars as above noted glean support for their views.

In the dual-account of the miraculous feeding (6:34-44 and 8:1-10), every point appears to reflect the celebration of the Lord's Supper in Mark's time. In 6:39 and 8:6 Jesus appears in the role of president or presiding officer of the "love feast" (a festive meal with which the Supper was originally connected, cf. 1 Cor. 11:17 ff.) and Supper. The disciples' distribution of the loaves and fish (6:41 and 8:6) as well as their gathering up of the fragments (6:43 and 8:8) corresponds to the duties assumed by the "deacons" in the primitive celebration. The blessing (6:41) or thanksgiving (8:6) and the breaking of the bread (6:41 and 8:6)—in both instances the Greek verbs are used from which the ancient church derived its technical terms for the special giving of thanks *(Eucharist)* and breaking of bread *(Klasis)* at the Supper—reflect such practices as have continued in Christian congregations to the present. The *Didache,* an ancient church manual of the second century, reads:

> Now about the Eucharist: This is how to give thanks: First in connection with the cup: "We thank you, our Father, for the holy vine of David, your child, which you have revealed through Jesus, your child

> To you be glory forever." Then in connection with the piece [broken off the loaf]: "We thank you, our Father, for the life and knowledge which you have revealed through Jesus, your child. To you be glory forever. As this piece [of bread] was scattered over the hills and then was brought together and made one,[12] so let your Church be brought together from the ends of the earth into your Kingdom. For yours is the glory and the power through Jesus Christ forever."[13]

Even the references to the hour of the day and the arrangement of the multitudes into companies of fifty and one hundred (6:35, 39-40) reflect ancient Christian practice, at least until the turn of the century when the Lord's Supper ceased to be an evening celebration. Mark's reference to the "green grass" upon which Jesus commands the groups to sit (6:39) might contain an allusion to the Western, Roman practice of celebrating the Supper at Passover—a springtime, April, festival.

One of the most interesting problems posed by Mark's sermon deals with his dating of Jesus' crucifixion and death. As noted earlier,[14] in his account of the Passion Mark pays uncharacteristic attention to detail. From the plot of the chief priests and scribes in 14:1 to the visit of the women to the tomb in 16:2 there are at least twelve references to the day or hour of the day (cf. 14:1, 2, 12, 17, 30; 15:1, 25, 33, 34, 42; 16:1, 2).[15] Mark's concentration upon the cross and death as constituting the heart and core of his sermon furnishes the fundamental reason for this meticulous regard for detail. But another, subordinate motive may be present here also. By means of careful attention to the temporal Mark may be confirming the practice of a part of the ancient church with regard to the commemoration of Jesus' dying and rising.

It will not be news to the reader that the accounts of Mark, Matthew, and Luke differ from that of the Fourth Gospel in the matter of the date of the crucifixion. According to the Fourth Evangelist Jesus was crucified on the day of Preparation, i.e., on Thursday, the 14th of the Jewish month Nisan (or Abib, the Hebrew term for our "ear of corn," thus denoting the month of plowing and sowing), the first month in the Jewish calendar. In other words, the Fourth Gospel dates Jesus' crucifixion one day before the Passover was actually eaten, when the lambs were slaughtered (cf. John 13:1; 18:28; 19:14, 31, 42). Thus the Fourth Evangelist sets the events of the Passion one day earlier than Mark (hence also Matthew and Luke), for whom the crucifixion takes place precisely at Passover, or on Friday, the fifteenth of the month Nisan.

The debate concerning which of the two accounts is to be preferred, synoptic or Johannine, will no doubt rage till doom's day. Our interest, however, lies elsewhere. For centuries the church of the West, following the synoptic tradition of Jesus' Friday crucifixion, has observed the Passion on "Good Friday." To this observance may be traced the hebdomadal or Friday fasts traditional within the liturgical denominations of Western Christianity. In churches of the East, and particularly in Asia Minor and Syria, Christians once observed the crucifixion on the *quarta decima,* that is, on the 14th day of the first month in the Jewish calendar, and regardless of the day in the week. (The reader will remember that the Jewish calendar was essentially a lunar calendar, and unlike our solar or Julian calendar contained roughly only 354 days in the year, for which reason a birthday or festival would not fall on the same day of the week each year. In order for such to occur, the intercalation of an additional month every leap year would be required.) The title *Quartodecimans* or "Fourteeners" thus came to be applied to such groups.[16]

Now the mere fact that Mark's dates coincide with Western Good Friday observance proves nothing. But suppose we were to light upon a passage or two which appeared to indicate another date for the crucifixion, a time-reference which appeared to contradict the sequence Mark normally follows and which he might be assumed to have "suppressed" in the interests of liturgical practice? In my opinion, chapter 14:1-2 furnishes precisely such an instance:

> It was now two days before the Passover and the feast of Unleavened Bread. And the chief priests and the scribes were seeking how to arrest him by stealth, and kill him; for they said, "Not during the feast, lest there be a tumult of the people."

If, upon Mark's own admission in 14:12 we understand the first day of Unleavened Bread to refer to the day on which the lambs were slain (i.e., Thursday, the 14th of Nisan) and reckon two days backward from this point, the death-plot was originally hatched on Tuesday, the 12th of Nisan. Jesus then held the last supper with his disciples on Wednesday the 13th and was crucified on the Thursday following. The passage just quoted clearly contradicts the actual course of Mark's Passion narrative. To ease the difficulty, a host of biblical scholars prefer to give a looser interpretation to the time-reference in 14:1-2, or contend that Judas' offer to betray Jesus stimulated his enemies, in contrast to their original intent, to act publicly and precipitously. In light of Mark's definition of the day of Unleavened Bread in 14:12 and in view of the danger of arguing a position which has no support in the text, such explanations are highly suspect.

In 15:42-43 we encounter another time-reference which contradicts Mark's usual sequence:

> And when evening had come, since it was the day of Preparation, that is, the day before the sabbath, Joseph of Arimathea, a respected member of the council, who was also himself looking for the kingdom of God, took courage and went to Pilate, and asked for the body of Jesus.

Since the Jewish day began at sundown, or at approximately 6:00 p.m., the reference in 15:42 is to the onset of Friday, the 15th of Nisan, the crucifixion thus having occurred on Thursday.

Such references as these are traces of another, older tradition which Mark did not altogether erase. They are in such apparent contrast to the balance of his Passion story as to raise the suspicion that the sequence which Mark generally follows is a reflection of Western, anti-quartodeciman practice with respect to the observance of "Good Friday" and Easter, a sequence which he sought to superimpose upon the older account.

These examples which appear to reflect the faith and practice of Mark's community ought further to convince the reader of the sermonic character of his Gospel. It is clearly Mark's intent not merely to set down the memorabilia of Jesus, but to reflect in Jesus' history the confession of the Christian company as well as to find in that history the life and experience of that company described and even prophesied. From this standpoint, the alleged abrupt ending of Mark's Gospel has a remarkable appropriateness about it.[17] Once Christ's victory had been announced in the angel's word—"Do not be amazed; you seek Jesus of Nazareth, who was crucified. He has risen" (16:6)—could there be any doubt as to the ultimate outcome? That fellowship which he had "created to be with him" (3: 14), which had become partaker of the "new covenant" (14:24), had already been given a share in the life of the Conqueror. What lay ahead in the not so far distant future would not be an addition or supplement to what the community had received—it would follow from it as an inevitable consequence. For that reason, once the announcement of victory had been made, there was nothing more to tell—Christ's future as well as the future of his community had already been described. Of far greater importance, however, is the fact that Mark is not obliged to add the appearances of Jesus as a separate item or appendix to the announcement of his resurrection because of the conviction that the "word" he proclaimed was the gospel of the risen, exalted Lord, alive and present in the community to which he proclaimed it. In that sense, the entire Gospel of Mark constitutes a post-resurrection appearance. For it is true of our preacher above all that his passion lies not in who Jesus was, but rather in who he *is*.

These community reflections in Mark are thus no mere benediction pronounced upon the church's beliefs, institutions and rituals, no mere attempt to give legitimacy to the developing structure by trajecting later opinion into the mouth of the so-called "historical Jesus" so as to make him its author. The reflections are a translation of the gospel into the life and needs of Mark's contemporaries. In this sense they share a common purpose with the "secret" and serve to make Mark's Gospel a Gospel.

Epilogue

One Last Look at the Preacher

It is time now to attempt some description of our preacher. The oldest tradition concerning Mark is that of Papias:[1]

> The elder also said this: Mark, who was the interpreter of Peter, wrote down accurately, though not in [chronological] sequence, everything he remembered which had been said or done by the Lord. For he neither heard nor followed the Lord, but later, as I said [heard and followed] Peter who delivered his lectures according to need, but not as though giving an arrangement of the words of the Lord. So that Mark did not err when he wrote something down as he remembered it. For he took thought for one thing, neither to omit the things he heard nor to falsify anything in them.[2]

These comments contain not only the witness of "the elder," but also (beginning with the second sentence) Papias' own evaluation of his informant's comment. What "the elder" says about Mark is that he stood close to Peter as his "go-between" (the word "interpreter" here is probably not to be taken in the usual sense of the term—dragoman or translator—but as referring to

Mark's transmitting in written form the content of Peter's reminiscences).

"The elder" further notes that Mark carefully penned the remembrances of Peter; that he proceeded in exact fashion, though in the chronological arrangement of the words and deeds of Jesus he deviated from the usual historical outline. If "the elder" referred to is John, son of Zebedee, apostle of the Lord, his judgments on Mark's Gospel are easy to explain—Mark's reminiscences are complete, though his Gospel offers only the words and deeds of Jesus contained in Peter's lectures. In other words, Mark's arrangement deviates from the outline of events as "the elder" remembers it and describes it in the Fourth Gospel. But it is not at all certain that Papias refers here to the Apostle John. Indeed, from his comments on the authorship of the Fourth Gospel, it is possible that between Papias and the son of Zebedee there stands not only the unnamed "elder," but another group of witnesses from whom Papias inquired as to what "the elder" might have said concerning the teaching of his predecessor—the original disciple of Jesus! Further, "the elder's" description of Mark's Gospel as bearing the immediate stamp of Peter does not stand up under careful scrutiny. Mark's particular point of view does not point to any early apostolic or Petrine tradition, but rather to his own independent conception. Yet, the fact that Matthew and Luke are so dependent upon Mark suggests that some kind of apostolic authority may stand behind his work.

The Muratorian Canon, a Latin fragment from the beginning of the third century, contained in a seventh- or eighth-century manuscript discovered in the Ambrosian Library at Milan, appears to indicate[3] that Mark was present at certain events which he records and that he described them as he experienced them. Justin Martyr, who ended his career at Rome, calls Mark's Gospel "the reminiscences of Peter." Clement of Alexandria (third century), whose "sketches" or "outlines" are, together with Papias' comments, also preserved in Eusebius' *Ecclesiastical History*[4] writes that Mark, companion of Peter, was asked to write down the content of the apostle's preaching. When Peter heard of it, he neither hindered nor encouraged Mark. From these few references it is plain to see that the "church fathers" displayed an ever-increasing tendency to place our preacher in intimate connection with Peter and thus to attribute to his Gospel an apostolic origin. But at the bottom of it all lies the shaky footing of Papias' comment, capable of myriad interpretations.

Despite the tenuous character of the tradition, however, there is no reason why we may not identify the Mark of Papias *et al* with the oft-named John Mark of the New Testament. According to Acts 12:12 he was the son of a certain Mary, in whose house a part of the early Jerusalem congregation gathered. His uncle, Barnabas (cf. Col. 4:10), together with Paul took him to Antioch after the collection trip noted in Acts 12:25 as well as on the so-called "first missionary journey" (Acts 13:5). On this occasion, Mark proved unreliable (Acts 13:13). On his account, Barnabas separated from Paul at Antioch and took Mark to Cyprus (Acts 15:37 ff.). Later, Mark rejoined the Pauline circle. In Philemon 24 Paul speaks of him as a "fellow worker," and in Colossians 4:10 commends him to the congregation at Colossae. (The author of 2 Timothy requests Timothy to bring Mark with him to Rome because of his usefulness, 4:11.) According to 1 Peter 5:13, Mark was with Peter in "Babylon," i.e., Rome. The statement of Papias to the effect that Mark was not a hearer or follower of the Lord can be harmonized with the notice of the Muratorian Canon that Mark was present at a few of the scenes which he describes. Accordingly, Mark may have grown up in Jerusalem and thus have experienced the final events in the life of Jesus. Some have suggested that the episode in Mark 14:51-52 reflects our preacher's first-hand experience:

> And a young man followed him, with nothing but a linen cloth about his body; and they seized him, but he left the linen cloth and ran away naked.

Do we have here an Alfred Hitchcock type self-portrait, deftly squeezed into the drama in place of a monogram? We have no way of telling whether or not Mark has inserted a "personal reference" into his sermon here, but the idea has captivated many scholars.[5]

The Monarchian Prologue to the Gospel (beginning of the third century) describes Mark as a Levite. This is a possibility, inasmuch as Barnabas was also a Levite (Acts 4:36). The same Prologue records that Mark carried on a priestly function, but following his conversion to the faith cut off his thumb so as to disqualify himself for priestly service. Hence the nickname "Colybodactylus," "stubby-fingered." It is doubtful, however, whether or not this epithet which appears in the older Anti-Marcionitic Prologue (A.D. 160-180) refers to some bodily peculiarity or to the sermon of Mark itself.[6] According to subsequent tradition, our preacher was the first bishop of Alexandria.

Regarding the time of the Gospel's composition, the Gospel itself contains no trace of late origin. Since in chapter 13 the destruction of Jerusalem is nowhere presupposed (13:14 refers only to the imminent desecration of the temple), Mark undoubtedly penned his sermon before the year A.D. 70, the year of the sack of Jerusalem and the temple ruin at the hands of the Roman general Titus. The period between A.D. 63 and 70 is as good as any other within which to fix the composition of the Gospel.

Notes

Chapter 1

[1]On this subject, cf. pp. 85 ff.

[2]*Early Christian Fathers, The Library of Christian Classics,* translated and edited by Cyril C. Richardson (Philadelphia: The Westminster Press, 1953), I, 382.

[3]I use the words "kind" and "type" advisedly, since no literary dependence of Mark upon Paul can be demonstrated.

Chapter 2

[1]Cf. Papias' statement on p. 113.

[2]Cf. the Old Testament parallel to 1:24 and 5:7 in 1 Kings 17:18.

[3]The reader will glean some illumination on this feature of Jesus' activity by referring to the experiences of Johann Christoph Blumhardt as noted in Rudolf Otto, *The Kingdom of God and the Son of Man,* translated by Floyd V. Filson and Bertram Lee-Woolf (Boston: Star King Press, 1957), pp. 346 ff.

[4]Cf., for example, such features as Jesus' rebuke in chapter 4, "Why are you afraid? Have you no faith?" (v. 40), and his word of comfort in chapter 5, "Take heart, it is I; have no fear" (v. 50), with the "young man's" word and subsequent events in chapter 16: "And he said to them, 'Do not be amazed . . . .' . . . And they went out and fled from the tomb; for trembling and astonishment had come upon them; and they said nothing to any one, for they were afraid" (16:6, 8).

[5]"It is not right to take the children's bread and throw it to the dogs. . . . 'Yes, Lord; yet even the dogs under the table eat the children's crumbs' " (7:27-28).

[6]Cf. pp. 24 f.

[7]Fulton Oursler, *The Greatest Story Ever Told* (Garden City, N.Y.: Doubleday and Co., 1963), p. 94.

[8]According to the usual pointing of the Greek text, I punctuate 1:27 as follows: ". . . they questioned among themselves, saying, 'What is this? A new teaching with authority; he commands even the unclean spirits, and they obey him.' "

[9]*D. Martin Luthers Werke,* 47. Band (Weimar: Hermann Böhlaus Nachfolger, 1912), 340, 27-33.

[10]See p. 15.

[11]*Theologisches Wörterbuch zum Neuen Testament,* ed. Gerhard Kittel, (Stuttgart: Kohlhammer, 1935), II, 23.

[12]Ernst Lohmeyer, *Das Evangelium des Markus, Kritisch-exegetischer Kommentar über das Neue Testament,* 11. Auflage (Göttingen: Vandenhoeck und Ruprecht, 1951), p. 320.

[13]"Crito: Socrates in Prison," *The Works of Plato,* trans. by B. Jowett (New York: Tudor Publishing Company, n.d.), pp. 144, 157

[14]Only Luke and John suggest that Jesus' hands were nailed to the cross; cf. Luke 24:39 and John 20:24-29.

[15]Sanhedrin 6.4, lines 50-65, quoted by C. K. Barrett, *The New Testament Background: Selected Documents* (New York: Harper and Row, 1961), p. 172.

[16]Cf. p. 20.

[17]Do Luke and John find this utterance so intolerable that the one substitutes for it a quotation from Psalm 31:5 (Luke 23:46) and the other the words "It is finished" (John 19:30)?

[18]The reader will note that in the RSV, vv. 9-20 together with a variant of v. 8, appear in italics and smaller print, so as to denote their questionable authenticity.

[19]Named for an obscure figure cited by Papias of Hierapolis (at first or second hand?) as an authority on the composition of the Gospels, called "Aristo" in an Armenian text of the Gospels, and thus perhaps confused with Aristo of Pella who may or may not have been a Christian!

[20]Adolf Jülicher, *Einleitung in das Neue Testament, Siebente Auflage* (Tübingen: J. C. B. Mohr, 1931), p. 311.

[21]We noted one instance in which an apologetic motif may be present in Mark, i.e., 15:42 ff. (cf. pp. 35 f.), and which could be directed against the argument that Jesus only appeared to be dead, but in reality was not and hence appeared to his disciples as risen.

[22]W. A. 17, I, 183, 10; 192, 12. Cf. also the discussion of the resurrection in connection with "community reflections" on pp. 106 ff.

[23]Ernst Käsemann, "Kritische Analyse von Phil. 2, 5-11," *Exegetische Versuche und Besinnungen* (Göttingen: Vandenhoeck und Ruprecht, 1960), I, 84.

[24]Käsemann, *op. cit.*, p. 85

[25]Cf. pp. 74 ff.

[26]Cf. p. 27.

[27]Cf. Vincent Taylor, *The Gospel According to St. Mark* (London: Macmillan and Co., 1955), p. 154.

[28]Cf. pp. 24 f.

[29]Käsemann, *op. cit.*, p. 86.

[30]Adolf Deissmann, *Light From the Ancient East,* translated by Lionel R. M. Strachan (London: Hodder and Stoughton, 1910), p. 257, italics mine.

Chapter 3

[1]"He who sent me to baptize with water said to me, 'He on whom you see the Spirit descend and remain, this is he who baptizes me with the Holy Spirit.' And I have seen and have borne witness that this is the Son of God" (John 1:33-34).

[2]Considerable controversy has raged over the question as to whether or not Jesus' injunctions to silence are to be regarded as redactionary, i.e., as originating with Mark. One scholar suggests

that such commands as appear in 1:44; 5:43; 7:36 and 8:26 were already present in the tradition which Mark appropriated, and for the purpose of defending Jesus against the charge of being a magician. Anton Fridrichsen, "Le probleme du miracle dans le Christianisme primitif," Etudes d'histoire et de philosophie religieuses XII (1925), 77 ff.

[3]In the Greek of 1:34 and 3:11-12 the imperfect tense of the verb is used, which suggests that Jesus habitually enjoined the demons to silence.

[4]Other passages in which this title occurs are: 2:10, 28; 8:31, 38; 9:9, 12, 31; 10:33, 45; 13:26; 14:21 (twice), 41, 62.

[5]It would be profitable and interesting to follow up Mark's almost schematic use of interrogatives, to determine the degree to which they heighten the question of Jesus' identity.

[6]Very often Mark's reference to Jesus' entering a "house" serves the idea of the secret. For example, in 7:17 Jesus enters a house, i.e. "leaves the people"; cf. also 2:1; 9:28, etc.

[7]Here, as in chapter 4, the quotation from Isaiah 6 suggests that the disciples' misunderstanding also has its ground in the divine will: ". . . Do you not yet perceive or understand? Are your hearts hardened? Having eyes do you not see, and having ears do you not hear? . . ." (vv. 17b-18).

[8]Here the title is used as a personal pronoun, i.e., "I."

[9]Cf. this greeting with Psalm 118:25-26.

[10]*Saint Justin Martyr, The Fathers of the Church* (New York: Christian Heritage, Inc., 1948), p. 208.

[11]*Ibid.*, p. 291.

[12]Cf. p. 77.

[13]T. A. Burkill, *Mysterious Revelation* (New York: Cornell University Press, 1963), p. 322.

[14]Wilhelm Wrede, *Das Messiasgeheimnis in den Evangelien* (Göttingen: Vandenhoeck und Ruprecht, 1901), pp. 125 f.

[15]Wrede, *op. cit.*, pp. 127 f.

[16]The healing of Bartimaeus just referred to (p. 85) aptly illustrates Mark's point of view, and appears to anticipate the theme of John 9:39, that the Lord has come "that those who do not see may see, and that those who see may become blind."

[17]Wrede, *op. cit.*, pp. 129 ff.

[18]Søren Kierkegaard, *Philosophical Fragments,* translated by David F. Swenson (Princeton: Princeton University Press, 1944), p. 25; cf. pp. 20 ff.

[19]Cf. Käsemann, *op. cit.*, p. 82.

Chapter 4

[1]Cf. pp. 22 f.

[2]Cf. p. 29 f.

[3]See p. 16.

[4]*Didascalia Apostolorum,* The Syriac Version Translated and Accompanied by the Verona Latin Fragments, With an Introduction and Notes by R. Hugh Connolly (Oxford: At the Clarendon Press, 1929), p. 180; cf. p. 189.

[5]Is the reference to Simon of Cyrene, father of Alexander and Rufus (members of Mark's community?), who carried Jesus' cross, intended to symbolize this requirement of faith? Cf. 15:21

[6]Willi Marxsen, *Der Evangelist Markus,* Studien zur Redaktionsgeschichte des Evangeliums (Göttingen: Vandenhoeck und Ruprecht, 1956).

[7]Benjamin W. Bacon, *Is Mark a Roman Gospel?* (Cambridge: Harvard University Press, 1919), p. 69.

[8]Cf. n. 3, p. 119.

[9]Philip Carrington, *The Primitive Christian Calendar,* A Study in the Making of the Marcan Gospel (Cambridge: At the University Press, 1952).

[10]Philip Carrington, *According to Mark,* A Running Commentary on the Oldest Gospel (Cambridge: At the University Press, 1960).

[11]John Bowman, *The Gospel of Mark,* The New Christian Jewish Passover Haggadah (Leiden: E. J. Brill, 1965).

[12]Does this phrase hint at Mark 6:34: "he had compassion on them, because they were like sheep without a shepherd . . . "? If so, the prayer of the *Didache* has a verbal connection with the feeding of the five thousand.

[13]*Early Christian Fathers, The Library of Christian Classics,* Cyril C. Richardson ed. (Philadelphia: The Westminster Press, 1953), I, 175.

[14]Cf. p. 15.

[15]Cf. p. 45.

[16]When the Western church fixed the celebration of Easter in conjunction with the solar calendar, the Quartodecimans were excommunicated for "Judaizing."

[17]Cf. the earlier discussion of the resurrection on pp. 60 ff.

Epilogue

[1]Cf. p. 14.

[2]Translated from the Greek fragment contained in Huck-Lietzmann's *Synopsis of the First Three Gospels,* 9th ed. (New York: American Bible Society, 1935), p. vii.

[3]The Fragment seems to begin with a line on the composition of Mark's Gospel.

[4]Cf. Huck-Lietzmann, *op. cit.,* p. ix.

[5]Cf. an analogous reference to Simon of Cyrene, father of Alexander and Rufus (members of Mark's community?) in 15:21.

[6]Cf. p. 12.

Index of Bible Passages

Mark

2